ALL ABOUT
CHICKEN

ALL ABOUT
CHICKEN

IRMA S. ROMBAUER
MARION ROMBAUER BECKER
ETHAN BECKER

PHOTOGRAPHY BY LEIGH BEISCH

SCRIBNER
NEW YORK · LONDON · TORONTO · SYDNEY · SINGAPORE

Scribner
1230 Avenue of the Americas
New York, NY 10020

WELDON OWEN INC.
Chief Executive Officer: John Owen
President: Terry Newell
Chief Operating Officer: Larry Partington
Vice President, International Sales: Stuart Laurence
Publisher: Roger Shaw
Creative Director: Gaye Allen
Associate Publisher: Val Cipollone
Art Director: Jamie Leighton
Production Director: Stephanie Sherman
Designer: Fiona Knowles
Consulting Editors: Norman Kolpas, Judith Dunham
Assistant Editor: Anna Mantzaris
Studio Manager: Brynn Breuner
Pre-press Coordinator: Mario Amador
Production Manager: Chris Hemesath
Food Stylist: Dan Becker
Prop Stylist: Sara Slavin
Studio Assistant: Sheri Giblin
Food Styling Assistant: Jonathan Justus
Step-by-Step Photographer: Chris Shorten
Step-by-Step Food Stylist: Kim Brent

Joy of Cooking All About series was designed
and produced by Weldon Owen Inc.,
814 Montgomery Street, San Francisco,
California 94133

Set in Joanna MT and Gill Sans

Separations by Bright Arts Singapore
Printed in Singapore by Tien Wah Press (Pte.) Ltd.

10 9 8 7 6 5 4 3 2 1

Library of Congress Cataloging-in-Publication Data
is available.

ISBN 0-7432-0204-X

Recipe shown on half-title page: *Grill-Smoked Jamaican Jerk Chicken*, 108
Recipe shown on title page: *Tandoori Chicken*, 108

CONTENTS

FOREWORD

"The chicken is a world-citizen," my Granny Rom wrote some seven decades ago in the first edition of the Joy of Cooking. Her words are even truer today. Few other main-course foods are as universally embraced and adapt so deliciously to the cooking styles of numerous countries and cultures.

Now, chicken stars in a volume of the new All About series. All About Chicken offers tips for buying and storing chicken, information on key ingredients, and recipes for marinades, stuffings, sauces, and gravies—everything you need whether you're cooking a casual supper or a holiday meal.

You might notice that this collection of kitchen-tested recipes is adapted from the latest edition of the Joy of Cooking. Just as our family has done for generations, we have worked to make this version of Joy a little bit better than the last. As a result, you'll find that some notes, recipes, and techniques have been changed to improve their clarity and usefulness. Since 1931, the Joy of Cooking has constantly evolved. And now, the All About series has taken Joy to a whole new stage, as you will see from the beautiful color photographs of finished dishes and clearly illustrated instructions for preparing and serving them. Granny Rom and Mother would have been delighted.

I'm sure you'll find All About Chicken to be both a useful and an enduring companion in your kitchen.

Enjoy!

Ethan Becker pictured with his grandmother, Irma von Starkloff Rombauer (left), and his mother, Marion Rombauer Becker (right). Irma Rombauer published the first Joy of Cooking at her own expense in 1931. Marion Rombauer Becker became coauthor in 1951. Joy as it has progressed through the decades (from top left to bottom right): the 1931 edition with Marion's depiction of St. Martha of Bethany, said to be the patron saint of cooking, "slaying the dragon of kitchen drudgery"; the 1943 edition; the 1951 edition; the 1962 edition; the 1975 edition; and the 1997 edition.

About Chicken

Chickens vary in size, from a 1-pound poussin to a 10-pound capon. As a general rule, figure on 1 pound chicken per person.

On the small end of the scale are the poussin (**1**) and the rock Cornish hen (**2**). Poussins, which are also called squab broilers (not to be confused with squab, a game bird), are simply very young chickens. Rock Cornish hens are a crossbreed of white Plymouth Rock and Cornish strains. Regardless of their lineage, they taste like all other chickens. At a diminutive 1 pound apiece, poussins may eventually displace rock Cornish hens as the birds of choice for single-serving presentation. Poussins are expensive and, in some areas, are available only through butchers or mail order. Rock Cornish hens used to run about 1¼ pounds, a perfect size for an individual serving, but for eco-

nomic reasons, producers are now bringing them to market in the 1½- to 1¾-pound range. Choose the smallest rock Cornish hens you can find when you want to serve one per person. A large rock Cornish hen, either roasted whole or split and broiled, makes a perfect dinner for two persons of modest appetite.

Today, most chickens weighing 2 to 3¼ pounds are sold to restaurants. What is left for supermarket sale are chickens at the heavier end of the midsized range, weighing between 3½ and 4¾ pounds (**3**). Usually these are labeled simply "whole chicken." If you do see one called a broiler/fryer, it probably will turn out to be a fairly large chicken like all the rest. If you are buying a whole midsized chicken for roasting, assume that it will feed four people, generously if it weighs over 4 pounds, modestly if it weighs

less. If you are buying the chicken to cut up and broil or fry, try to find one weighing 3½ pounds or less.

Large chickens—generally those weighing 5 to 7 pounds, though some producers include chickens weighing as little as 4 pounds in this category—are marketed today as roasting chickens or roasters (**4**). They are often perfect candidates for roasting (allow 1 pound per person), but they can also be cut up and baked, fricasseed, or stewed. But do not broil or fry them, for they will char on the outside before cooking through.

A capon (**5**) is a castrated young male chicken. His loss causes him to swell to a weight of 8 to 10 pounds, enough for eight or more generous servings. Traditionally, these birds are fed milk and bread the last ten days before processing, making their meat extremely white

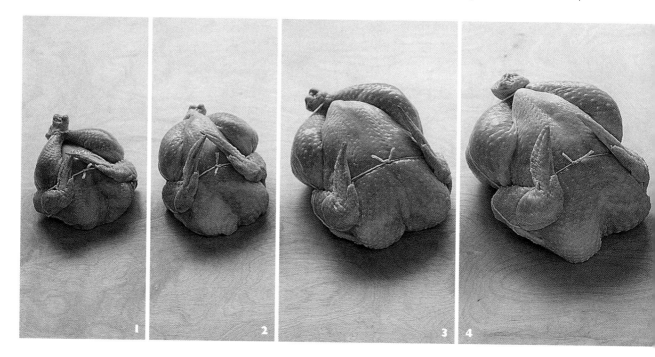

and tender. Capons come to the supermarket only at holiday time but are available through a butcher year-round.

There are two types of stewing hen, also called fowl: those that are raised for eggs, and those that are raised to lay eggs for hatching. The former are a leaner breed and, when slaughtered for sale as meat, used to be called "light" stewing hens. In recent years, these hens have been genetically redesigned to be even leaner, and, therefore, are no longer sold for meat at the retail level. The hatchers, formerly known as "heavy" stewing hens, still come to market as dressed whole birds. Stewing hens are much too tough to roast. The usual treatment is to stew them slowly, but, no matter how they are cooked, the meat is dry and distinctly stringy. Stewing hens make excellent stock and soup.

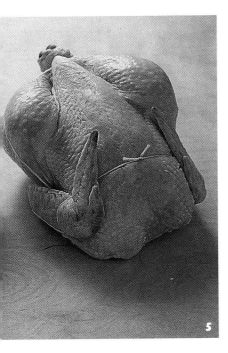

CHICKEN PRODUCTION

With the emergence of the modern chicken farm after World War II, chicken became increasingly affordable, everyday food. Unfortunately, as chicken production moved from the barnyard to the processing plant, both the quality and the safety of our chicken were compromised. In order to remain profitable in a highly competitive industry, producers rush their chickens to market less than forty days after hatching, which is simply not enough time for the birds to develop flavor. In addition, producers raise their chickens in crowded, sometimes squalid, conditions. To prevent the spread of disease, most add antibiotics to the feed, the long-term effects of which on consumers are unknown. And while antibiotics stave off epidemics in the coop, they do not kill off some infections, such as salmonellosis, quickly spread by overcrowding.

In response to the problems associated with mass production, a secondary industry has emerged, providing the consumer with "free-range," "organic," and "natural" chicken. These terms can be confusing, and some producers, intentionally or not, use them in ways that can be misleading.

By USDA standards, free-range chickens must have ready access to the out-of-doors. This does not mean that the birds roam freely. A free-range chicken is often one that has lived out its life in a coop with a single door leading to a small enclosed pen. Free-range chickens are not necessarily fed an organic diet. All "organic" chickens are, by law, free-range and must be allowed access to the outdoors. They must also be raised on an organic farm beginning no later than their second day of life and must be fed on feed that is 100 percent organically produced. Treatment with approved vaccines is allowed, as is the feeding of vitamin and mineral supplements. Hormones and antibiotics are prohibited.

The USDA's definition of the term "natural" is extremely broad. Any minimally processed bird can be called "natural," regardless of what it has been fed or how it has been raised. This means that only such products as precooked marinated chicken parts and additive-injected "self-basting" birds are excluded. Any other poultry product—from a premium poussin nurtured by a small producer to an ordinary supermarket package of boneless, skinless chicken breasts—can be labeled "natural" by USDA definitions. But some producers mean something more specific by the term. Some define a "natural" chicken as one that was fed a pesticide-free, antibiotic-free diet, much like an organic chicken. Others call a bird "natural" if it tests antibiotic-free at slaughter, which may be accomplished by withdrawing antibiotics from the chicken's feed ten days before processing.

Kosher chickens are processed according to Jewish dietary laws. Rabbis supervise their production and perform the ritual slaughtering. After slaughter, the chickens undergo a three-hour process of cold-water defeathering, soaking, brining, and drying that is designed to draw out as much blood as possible. The salt used in brining permeates the bird, causing the cooked meat to taste pleasantly seasoned.

To serve the Muslim population, halal chickens are showing up in supermarkets across the country. Unlike ordinary supermarket chickens, halal chickens are hand-slaughtered by someone of the Islamic faith.

Buying Chicken

First and foremost, be sure to check the "sell by" date on the package. Don't buy chicken whose time is nearly up, unless you plan to eat it right away. If the package contains an unusual amount of liquid, feels sticky, or has even the faintest off-odor, the contents are suspect, regardless of what the expiration date may be. Avoid icy chicken. Since most poultry has already been frozen by the time it comes to the store, this has been, in effect, frozen twice, damaging texture and flavor.

The color of chicken skin is not an indication of quality. Rather, producers manipulate skin color through feed and processing in order to satisfy consumer preferences. Consumers in the Northeast have long preferred yellow-skinned chickens (above right). Producers in the South cater to their customers' predilection for pale, almost white

chickens (above left). As skinless parts become more the norm, skin color becomes less of an issue.

Most consumers assume that the chickens in their supermarket meat case are fresh, not frozen. Until recently, however, federal law permitted chicken and other birds to be "stored" at temperatures as low as 0°F and still be called "fresh." The law has been changed, but consumers are only slightly better off. Now, if it is to be labeled "fresh," poultry need only be stored at temperatures above 26°F, which means that it may arrive at the supermarket having been kept below 32°F, the freezing point, for several weeks before we buy it. The new law stipulates that poultry stored at temperatures between 0° and 26°F cannot be labeled either fresh or frozen. In other words, if the label on a package of chicken does not explicitly

claim that the contents are "fresh," the chicken may actually have been frozen at 0°F for an indefinite period and then thawed before being offered for sale. Is there any such thing as frozen chicken? Yes. According to current law, it is chicken that has been held at temperatures below 0°F.

Where does this leave the consumer? Since chicken tastes best when it has been stored for the shortest length of time, "fresh" is still the best, for even though fresh chicken, generally speaking, has been frozen, it has not been frozen for long. As for those chickens at the supermarket that are not labeled either fresh or frozen, you can be assured that most have been processed fairly recently, since the high demand for chicken ensures a rapid turnover.

Storing and Freezing Chicken

Chicken should be stored in the back of the refrigerator, where the temperature is coldest, and cooked and eaten within a day or two of purchase. Leave it in its original packaging. If chicken proves to have a slight off-odor when you open the package, it can be refreshed. Rinse it well under cool running water, then place it in a bowl with cold water to cover and add 1 tablespoon vinegar or lemon juice and 1 teaspoon salt for every cup of water. Refrigerate the chicken from 1 to 4 hours, then proceed with the recipe. Since the skin is especially prone to spoilage, it is advisable to remove it.

Any chicken that cannot be eaten promptly should be frozen. Leave it in its original packaging. (If the bird is wrapped in butcher's paper, leave it in the wrap and place it in a self-sealing plastic bag.) Assuming a freezer temperature of 0°F or lower, frozen chicken will remain safe to eat for a year or longer, but, for the best taste and texture, cook it within a month.

Frozen chicken must be thawed before cooking, either in the refrigerator or, for quicker results, in cold water. If thawing in the refrigerator, set the bird, still in its original packaging, on a baking sheet and defrost 1 day for every 6 pounds. If thawing in cold water, enclose the bird, in its original packaging, in a sealed plastic bag, place it in water, and weight it with a plate or pot to keep it submerged. Defrost for 1 to 8 hours, depending on weight, changing the water periodically. Chicken can appear to be thawed before it really is. Do not declare it fully defrosted until the flesh feels pliable and squashy to the touch and the legs and wings move freely at the joints when wiggled. In the case of birds that are to be roasted whole, under-thawing is disastrous, for the birds will cook through on the outside while the center remains virtually raw. Should a refrigerator-thawed whole bird prove to be stiff and icy on the day you plan to roast it, transfer it to cold water to finish defrosting.

Avoiding Contamination

Thawed chicken is highly susceptible to spoilage and must be cooked promptly. Unless you can be absolutely certain that it never reached a temperature above 40°F during thawing, do not refreeze. Most frozen processed birds—for example, already-stuffed whole birds—must be transferred directly from the freezer to a hot oven. Follow the package instructions to the letter. Contrary to popular belief, the undercooking of chicken is rarely the cause of salmonella illness. (Stuffed whole birds are an important exception.) Salmonella is seriously compromised at 140°F, a temperature at which chicken remains nearly raw, and is completely eradicated at 160°F, the lowest temperature to which most people would ever think of cooking a chicken, unless, for some odd reason, they liked the meat bloody. Rather, the usual way in which people contract a salmonella infection is by eating a raw or lightly cooked food that has come into contact with infected raw chicken or its juices. Remember that to reduce the chances of contamination, never store raw birds, even when wrapped, next to an unwrapped food that will be eaten raw, such as salad greens or bread. And after cutting up or otherwise handling raw chicken, be sure to always wash your hands, cutting board, counter surface, knives, poultry shears, and so on, in hot sudsy water before preparing another food.

Cutting Up Chicken

Using a reasonably sharp knife, any home cook can easily cut a whole chicken into serving pieces with just a little practice. By cutting up a bird yourself, you not only save a considerable amount of money but also ensure that you will have precisely the right parts, cut just the way you want them. Of course, for most cooks, the parts available at the supermarket will do just fine, but the supermarket does not always provide for special needs. Supermarkets never offer butterflied chickens, perfect for stuffing under the skin and roasting, and they rarely offer halved and quartered chickens, which are nice grilled or broiled. Supermarkets detach the "oysters," the delicious nuggets of meat that lie on either side of the small of the back, from the thighs, and they jumble large and small parts from different chickens together in the same pack, which creates problems for a cook who wants to broil or fry, techniques that require small parts.

The back, neck, heart, and gizzard from a cut-up bird will make 2 to 3 cups of excellent stock. (See our recipe for *Chicken Stock*, 124.) These pieces can all be wrapped and frozen for future use.

HOW TO CUT UP A CHICKEN

This is how one makes so-called chicken parts. Generally speaking, chickens are cut into six pieces: two whole legs, two whole wings, and two breast halves. To make eight pieces, cut the thighs from the drumsticks. To make an additional two pieces, cut the breast halves in half again.

1 Start with the legs. Lay the bird on its side, pull the leg away from the body, and cut into the skin with the knife held close to the thigh so that you will not remove too much of the breast skin. As you cut, continue to pull up on the leg until the thighbone pops out of its socket.

Press the tip of a paring knife against the backbone just behind the thigh joint and dig out the little nugget of meat, called the oyster.

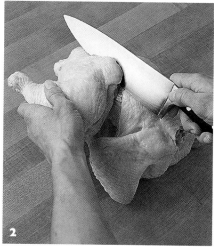

2 Slice through the skin from the tip of the oyster to the opposite corner of the thigh and detach the leg. If you wish, you can leave half or all of the tail attached to the thigh skin. Repeat with the other leg.

3 To separate the drumstick and thigh, flex the leg and crack the ball joint. Place the leg on a cutting board with the inner side facing up and cut exactly at the thin line of fat separating the drumstick and thigh.

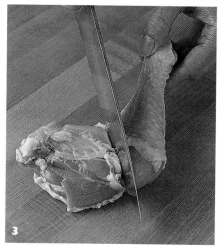

4 The wings can be removed at the joint or, to make a more ample serving, with a small piece of breast meat attached. To remove the wing at the joint, lay the chicken on its side, pull the wing away from the body until the joint is exposed, and cut.

To leave a piece of breast attached to the wing, lay the bird on its side and make a cut into the breast about 1 inch up from the top of the wing joint, parallel to the ribs. Pulling the wing away from the body, cut against the ribs until you reach the ball joint (left), then cut through the joint and detach the wing.

5 To separate the breast from the back, cut through the rib bones on either side of the backbone with poultry shears or a sharp knife. Be sure to cut close to the backbone, or you will lose the underside of the breast to the back. Reserve the back for stock.

Before cutting the breast, locate the wishbone at the thick end (opposite the cartilage tip), scrape it free from the surrounding flesh with the tip of a paring knife, and pull it out.

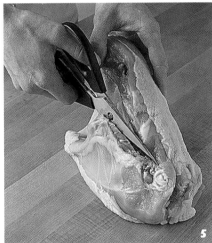

6 Stretch the breast skin smoothly over both halves of the breast, then turn the breast skin side down. Using a sharp knife, cut down the middle of the breast, through the reddish breastbone, to make two halves.

For some chicken dishes, you may want to cut the breast into 4 serving pieces. In order to do so, turn one breast half skin side up and, arching your free hand over the knife and stretching the skin between your fingers, cut the breast in half diagonally through the bone. (If you will be quartering the breast of a small chicken, you should remove the wings at or very near the joints, or else the back breast pieces will be rather bony.)

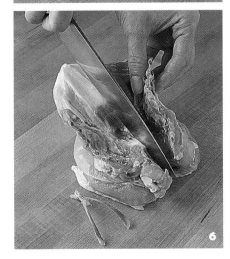

BUTTERFLYING OR SPLITTING A BIRD

To butterfly a bird, cut through the ribs on either side of the backbone and remove it (**1**). Turn the bird breast side up, place your palm over the breastbone, and press hard to flatten the bird (**2**).

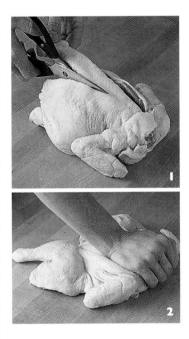

To split a bird, remove the backbone and flatten as for butterflying. Place the bird skin side down and pry out the reddish breastbone and attached cartilage. Cut the bird in half at the seam where the breastbone had been (**3**).

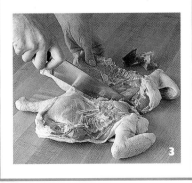

Chicken Parts

The remarks that follow pertain to standard chicken parts, which are cut from midsized chickens weighing 3¼ to just under 5 pounds.

MIXED PARTS

Even if a package of mixed chicken parts is labeled "whole cut-up chicken," the parts contained inside always come from a number of different chickens. So select packs whose parts look to be of more or less equal size. A leg from a 5-pound chicken will take much longer to cook than one from a 3½ pounder. Packages sometimes exclude parts, such as wings, that a consumer might expect to find.

QUARTERED CHICKEN

The idea behind quartering is to make four equal-sized servings of chicken. A quartered chicken consists of two breast halves, with the wings detached, and two whole legs. This combination is well suited to broiling. But sometimes a quartered chicken turns out to be a quartered breast, with the two front pieces attached to the legs and the two back pieces attached to the wings. Chicken cut in this way will not broil successfully but can be baked or braised.

BREAST

Chicken breast can be prepared in virtually any way imaginable. Just be very careful not to overcook it. As soon as the juices run clear when the meat is pricked with a fork, the breast is done.

Whole Chicken Breast: This is the whole breast of a chicken, with skin and bone attached. It can be roasted, broiled, baked, poached, or used to make a creamed dish, pot pie, or casserole. Split breasts can be used in the same ways as whole breasts and, because they are smaller, also can be braised or fried. Boneless chicken breasts come with the skin still attached but the bones removed. Although boneless chicken breasts can be used in the same ways as all other breasts, people usually buy these for broiling and grilling. The skin not only protects the meat during these heat-intensive procedures but also crisps up and chars slightly to delicious effect. Whole boneless chicken breasts can also be stuffed and folded over, the skin making a natural wrapping.

Boneless, Skinless Chicken Breasts: Also called chicken breast cutlets, chicken cutlets, or, in French, *suprêmes de volaille*, boneless, skinless chicken breasts are split chicken breasts with all skin and bone removed. Quick-cooking and low in fat, they are the most popular poultry cut in the United States. Boneless, skinless chicken breasts are most often sautéed or grilled over fairly high heat or poached and used to make chicken salad, pot pie, or casserole. However, they also can be cut into strips or bite-sized pieces before cooking and then stir-fried or skewered. Chicken breast "tenders" usually turn out to be boneless, skinless chicken breasts that have been cut into strips; not chicken breast tenderloins, which are the long, thin pieces of meat that lie beneath either side of the breast.

The important thing to remember about boneless, skinless chicken breasts is that they are easy to overcook. Cook them just to the point where they release clear juices when pricked with a fork, or they will be disappointingly dry and firm.

LEGS

Chicken legs are made up of not only the drumsticks but also the thighs. Unlike the breast, chicken legs are tolerant of long, thorough cooking, and are good for fricassees, stews, and other braised dishes. But legs take well to virtually any cooking treatment, including baking, broiling, frying, and grilling. Despite their firm texture and meaty flavor, legs do not appeal to most Americans.

In addition to whole chicken legs, supermarkets carry many kinds of leg parts. Chicken thighs are plumper and meatier than the drumsticks. Thighs take longer to cook than breasts, but otherwise they can be prepared in exactly the same ways. Chicken drumsticks are ideal for picnics or any other finger-food occasion. They take well to all cooking treatments, pan- or oven-frying in particular.

GROUND CHICKEN

Ground chicken comes in only one form; it is often labeled "lean" but actually has a fat content comparable to that of "regular" (7 to 10 percent fat) ground turkey. For many people, ground chicken makes a perfectly acceptable substitute for ground beef, particularly in highly seasoned dishes like chili and tacos. When substituting ground chicken for beef in mild dishes, you may want to increase the spice.

WINGS

Wings are available in three forms: whole, whole but with the tips removed, and first and second joints cut apart. Packs of mixed joints are often labeled "drumettes" or "buffalo wings," even though logically only the first joint can be considered a drumette. Wing tips are perfect for making stock.

BACK AND FEET

Chicken backs and feet are usually very inexpensive and good for stock. Rinse feet thoroughly before use. Hack or snip backs into 2-inch pieces with a chef's knife or heavy-duty kitchen shears before putting them into the pot. If the "oysters" are still attached to the backbone, you can pry them out and fry them.

GIZZARDS, HEARTS, AND LIVERS

These organs are referred to collectively as the giblets. Giblets are rarely cooked together except in the making of giblet gravy. Gizzards and hearts require long, slow braising in order to become tender. Chicken livers, by contrast, respond best to quick cooking and should be served while still pink and creamy on the inside.

HOW TO BONE AND SKIN A CHICKEN BREAST

Since boneless, skinless chicken breasts are very expensive, you may find it worth your time to bone and skin whole chicken breasts yourself.

1 Peel off the skin with your fingers. Locate the wishbone at the wide end of the breast (opposite the cartilage tip), scrape it free of the surrounding flesh with the tip of a paring knife, and pull it out. Place the breast skinned side up on your work surface and press down firmly with the heel of your hand to break the membrane covering the reddish breastbone and cartilage tip. Turn the breast over. Using the point of a paring knife, cut around the shoulder bones attached to the breastbone at the wide end of the breast and remove them. Free the breastbone and cartilage from the flesh with your fingers, then pull both out. Slip your fingers or a paring knife beneath the rib bones and work them free of the flesh.

2 Cut the breast in half at the breastbone line then trim any ragged edges.

3 You should remove the long white tendon that runs through each tenderloin, especially if it is thick. With the breast placed tenderloin side up, pull the thick end of the tenderloin away from the breast and lay it on your work surface. Holding the tip of the tendon down, scrape against the tendon with a knife until it detaches from the flesh. If you wish, reserve the bones and skin for making stock.

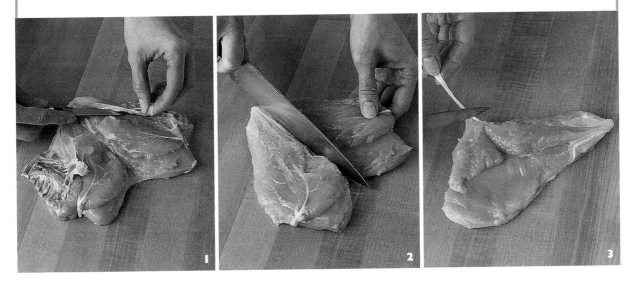

ABOUT
ROASTED
CHICKEN

*R*oasting a chicken does not require the skills of a restaurant chef. You will get perfectly good results if you proceed as your grandmother did. Simply arrange the chicken breast side up on a rimmed baking sheet or in a shallow roasting pan (deep pans interfere with browning) and roast it until the thigh releases clear juices when pricked with a fork. Our recipe for Roasted Chicken, 26, produces a bird that far surpasses the average take-out specimen.

If you are looking for perfection, you might consider trying the technique outlined in Turned Roasted Chicken, 27. This recipe calls for arranging the chicken on a rack (preferably a V-rack) and roasting it first on one side, then on the other, and finally breast side up. When a chicken is roasted on its sides, the dark meat is exposed to the reflected glare of the hot oven roof while the sensitive breast is turned toward the cooler oven walls. This serves to cook the dark meat at a faster rate than the breast, which is precisely what one wants, as the dark meat is done at an internal temperature of 170° to 180°F, while the white meat is cooked through at the much lower temperature of 160°F and begins to dry out and harden if heated much beyond 165°F. There is also gravity to consider. When a chicken sits breast side up throughout cooking, gravity inevitably draws the juices down toward the back and into the roasting pan. Flipping the chicken reverses the flow of the juices.

Casserole-Roasted Chicken with Forty Cloves of Garlic, 31

17

Trussing Chicken

Properly speaking, to truss a bird means to bind its legs and wings to the body, either by sewing through the joints with a trussing needle and twine or by simply tying the appendages into place. The closing of the body and neck cavities— which is necessary only if the bird is stuffed—is a separate procedure. Today, many people lump both operations under the rubric of "trussing," but when a recipe in this book calls for trussing, the binding of the bird, not the closing of the cavities, is what is meant. Trussing is rarely obligatory, but it does facilitate the handling of the bird, especially in those recipes that require turning during roasting, and it gives the bird a handsome shape.

REMOVING THE WISHBONE

You should remove the wishbone before you stuff, truss, or roast a whole bird. Doing so makes carving the whole roasted bird a neat and easy process.

Lift the skin of the raw bird at the neck end and, using the point of a paring knife, scrape against the wishbone until it is mostly freed from the surrounding flesh (**1**).

Hook the wishbone on either side with two fingers and pull it out (**2**). With the wishbone removed, you will be able to carve the breast of the cooked bird in unbroken slices.

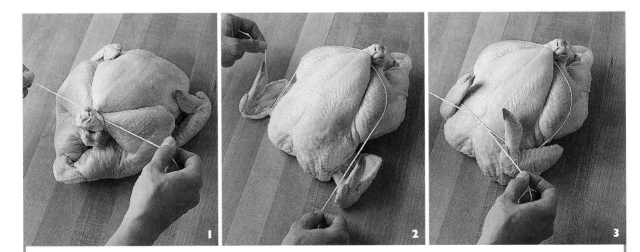

HOW TO TRUSS A CHICKEN

1 Cut a long piece of sturdy kitchen twine—about 18 inches long for rock Cornish hens and 30 inches long for chickens. Tie the center of the twine around the bird's ankles, binding the legs together.

2 Bring the ends of the twine over the backs of the legs and the lower breast. Loop the twine once around the wings at the elbow joint (that is, the joint between the two meaty parts of the wing).

3 Bring the ends of the twine over the lower third of the breast and tie them as tightly as possible. To complete the truss, tie a double knot in the twine and then trim the ends to a length of 1 inch.

Stuffing Chicken

In the past few years, stuffing, once considered by many to be the best part of the roasted bird, has acquired a controversial reputation. Some warn that stuffing can cause illness, that it soaks up fat, and that it causes the bird to overcook. Furthermore, they say, no one has the time, skill, or equipment necessary to stuff a bird properly. These voices miss the point. The whole purpose of stuffing is precisely to soak up the wonderfully flavorful juices that leach into a bird's cavity during roasting. We stress the word *juices*. The fat is in the skin. Chicken meat is lean, and it is the juices of the meat that the stuffing blots up. We will admit that stuffing presents its own challenges, but these are hardly insurmountable.

Most traditional stuffings begin with sautéed vegetables—always onions, usually celery, frequently bell peppers, and maybe garlic. Regional and personal preferences produce countless variations.

MAKING STUFFING AHEAD

All stuffings can be made ahead and refrigerated for up to 2 days. Stuffing intended to be baked inside a bird should be reheated before you stuff the bird with it. If making stuffing ahead, do not add any egg to the mixture until you have reheated it and are ready to stuff. The simplest method for reheating a stuffing is on top of the stove, stirring gently so as not to turn the whole mixture to mush. Stuffings to be baked in a dish can go directly from the refrigerator to the oven. Moisten it with stock before baking.

RULES FOR STUFFING BIRDS

● Always stuff the bird just before roasting—never ahead of time, which would give any harmful bacteria present in the cavity ample time to breed.

● Have the stuffing hot and pack it loosely in the body and neck cavities (**1**). The stuffing must reach a temperature of 160°F during roasting to ensure that any possible pathogens are killed. If it is cold and packed tightly, it will not heat to this point until long after the bird is done.

● You must close the cavities in order to keep the stuffing in place (**2**). The quickest and most efficient way to do this is by sewing the cavities shut with a trussing needle and twine. If you do not own a trussing needle, secure the body cavity with small skewers and lacing. Close the neck cavity with toothpicks.

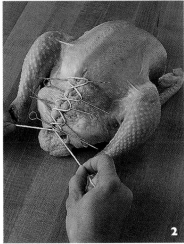

● When the bird has cooked through, take the temperature of the stuffing by plunging the stem of the thermometer deep into the body cavity (**3**). If the stuffing has not yet reached 160°F, take the bird out of the oven, scoop the stuffing into a buttered casserole, and bake while the bird stands before carving.

● Finally, always take all the stuffing out of the cooked bird as soon as you begin to carve. Stuffing left inside a bird may remain warm for several hours, providing a perfect environment for bacterial growth.

Basic Bread Stuffing

4 to 5 cups

This and the bread stuffing recipes that follow yield enough to stuff an oven roaster or 6 to 8 rock Cornish hens. Some of the variations yield enough for an additional small casserole of stuffing. The optional egg makes the stuffing firm. If you prefer the bread to be moist, skip the toasting step.

Position a rack in the center of the oven. Preheat the oven to 400°F. Toast until golden brown:

½ pound sliced firm white sandwich, French, or Italian bread, including crusts, cut into ½-inch cubes, or 5 cups lightly packed bread cubes

Turn into a large bowl. Heat in a large skillet over medium-high heat until the foam subsides:

2 to 4 tablespoons (¼ to ½ stick) unsalted butter

Add and cook, stirring, until tender, about 5 minutes:

1 cup chopped onions
½ cup finely chopped celery

Remove from the heat and stir in:

2 to 4 tablespoons minced fresh parsley
½ teaspoon dried sage, or 1½ teaspoons minced fresh
½ teaspoon dried thyme, or 1½ teaspoons minced fresh
½ teaspoon salt
¼ teaspoon ground black pepper
⅛ teaspoon freshly grated or ground nutmeg
Pinch of ground cloves

Stir into the bread cubes and toss until well combined. Depending on how much butter you started with and how firm you want the stuffing, stir in, a little at a time, until the stuffing is lightly moist but not packed together:

¼ to ½ cup Chicken Stock, 124
1 large egg, well beaten (optional)

Adjust the seasonings. To use as a stuffing, reheat just before spooning it into the bird(s). Or moisten with additional:

Stock and/or egg

Turn into a medium, shallow buttered baking dish. Bake in a 350°F oven until the top has formed a crust and the stuffing is heated through, 25 to 40 minutes.

BREAD STUFFING WITH TOASTED NUTS OR CHESTNUTS AND DRIED FRUIT

About 6 cups

Use shelled and roasted fresh chestnuts, or canned or frozen if desired; do not use chestnuts packed in syrup, which are too sweet for this dish. Prepare Basic Bread Stuffing, left, adding ¼ to ½ cup walnuts, pecans, or Brazil nuts, toasted and coarsely chopped, or ¾ cup chestnuts, boiled or toasted and coarsely chopped, and ¼ cup dried fruit, such as raisins, cranberries, cherries, or diced prunes, when tossing the bread with the seasonings.

BAKING STUFFING IN A DISH

Any remaining stuffing that does not fit into the cavity of the bird can be baked separately, or you may even prefer to bake all of the stuffing outside the bird. Stuffing baked outside the bird should first be moistened with ½ to 1 cup of stock, milk, or wine to make up for the missing juices that it would absorb when cooked inside a roasting bird.

Spread the stuffing in a shallow layer in a shallow buttered casserole or gratin dish. Ladle over enough stock, milk, or wine to moisten the stuffing, cover with aluminum foil if you wish, and bake in a preheated 350°F oven for 30 to 45 minutes. If you have covered the stuffing with aluminum foil but would like a crispy brown crust, dot the top with butter and bake uncovered for the last 20 minutes. If you are roasting a bird at the same time, baste the stuffing with pan drippings a few times during baking. If you plan to serve stuffing as the starchy side dish, allow about ¾ cup per person. Leftovers are always welcome.

Basic Corn Bread Stuffing

About 4 cups

Any corn bread will work in this recipe. However, if you are making corn bread from scratch, choose a recipe that is unsweetened. If you like the corn bread moist, skip the toasting step.

Position a rack in the center of the oven. Preheat the oven to 400°F. Toast until golden brown:

4 cups cubed corn bread

Turn into a large bowl. If you like a crumbly texture, break up the cubes with your fingers.

Heat in a large skillet over medium-high heat until the foam subsides:

2 to 4 tablespoons (¼ to ½ stick) unsalted butter

Add and cook, stirring, until tender, about 5 minutes:

1 cup chopped onions
½ cup finely chopped celery
½ green bell pepper, cut into small dice (optional)
½ red bell pepper, cut into small dice (optional)
1 clove garlic, minced (optional)

Remove from the heat and stir in:

2 to 4 tablespoons minced fresh parsley
½ teaspoon dried sage, or 1½ teaspoons minced fresh
½ teaspoon dried thyme, or 1½ teaspoons minced fresh
½ teaspoon salt
¼ teaspoon ground black pepper

Stir into the bread cubes and toss until well combined. Depending on how much butter you started with and how firm you want the stuffing, stir in, a little at a time, until the stuffing is lightly moist but not packed together:

¼ to ½ cup Chicken Stock, 124

1 large egg, well beaten (optional)

Adjust the seasonings. To use as a stuffing, reheat just before spooning it into the bird(s). Or moisten with additional:

Stock and/or egg

Turn into a medium, shallow buttered baking dish. Bake uncovered in a 350°F oven until the top has formed a crust and the stuffing is heated through, 25 to 40 minutes.

CORN BREAD STUFFING WITH SAUSAGE AND BELL PEPPERS

6 to 7 cups

Sausage and bell peppers are a hearty and robust combination.

Prepare *Basic Corn Bread Stuffing, above,* with the optional green and red bell peppers, adding ½ pound cooked hot or mild bulk sausage and, if desired, ⅛ teaspoon ground red pepper when tossing the bread with the seasonings.

CORN BREAD STUFFING WITH OYSTERS AND TOASTED PECANS

5 to 6 cups

Prepare *Basic Corn Bread Stuffing, above,* omitting the garlic and adding 1 dozen shucked (or ½ pint raw) oysters, drained, and/or ½ to 1 cup pecans, toasted and coarsely chopped, when tossing the bread with the seasonings. Use the drained oyster liquor in place of, or in addition to, the chicken stock.

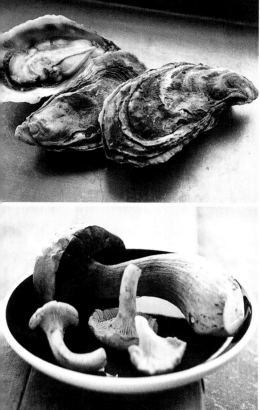

BREAD STUFFING WITH OYSTERS

About 6 cups

Try to use freshly shucked oysters.
Prepare *Basic Bread Stuffing, 20,*
adding 1 dozen shucked (or
½ pint raw) oysters, drained,
when tossing the bread with the
seasonings. Use the drained oyster liquor in place of, or in addition to, the chicken stock.

BREAD AND MUSHROOM STUFFING

5 to 6 cups

Heat 1 tablespoon unsalted
butter in a medium skillet over
medium-high heat until the foam
subsides. Add ½ pound mushrooms, wiped clean and sliced,
and cook, stirring, until tender and
the liquid is evaporated. Prepare
Basic Bread Stuffing, 20, adding the
cooked mushrooms when tossing
the bread with the seasonings.

Rice Stuffing with Almonds, Raisins, and Middle Eastern Spices

About 4 cups

*This intensely flavored stuffing goes well
with rock Cornish hens. Baked in a
casserole, it also makes a good side
dish with grilled chicken.*
Heat in a large skillet over medium
heat:

2 tablespoons olive oil
Add and cook, stirring, until tender,
about 5 minutes:
1 cup chopped onions
Add and stir until well coated:
1 tablespoon minced garlic
½ teaspoon ground cumin
½ teaspoon ground coriander
½ teaspoon ground turmeric
½ teaspoon sweet paprika
½ teaspoon ground ginger
½ teaspoon ground black pepper
¼ teaspoon salt
1 cup medium-grain rice

Stir in and bring to a simmer:
1½ cups Chicken Stock, 124
Reduce the heat to low, cover, and
simmer until the rice is cooked,
about 20 minutes. Turn the mixture
into a large bowl, let cool slightly,
and stir in:
¼ cup golden raisins
¼ cup diced pitted prunes
**¼ cup slivered blanched almonds,
toasted**
1 teaspoon grated lemon zest
2 tablespoons fresh lemon juice
1 large egg, lightly beaten
Adjust the seasonings. Use as a stuffing or turn into a large, shallow buttered baking dish, cover, and bake in
a 350°F oven until the flavors are
blended and the stuffing is hot,
20 to 30 minutes.

Mashed Potato Stuffing

5 to 6 cups

This surprisingly light stuffing, ideally made from leftover mashed potatoes, is excellent baked in a buttered casserole and served with roasted chicken—but it also makes a very good stuffing for capon.

Melt or heat in a large skillet over medium heat:

4 tablespoons (½ stick) unsalted butter or olive oil

Add and cook, stirring occasionally, until tender and beginning to caramelize, 10 to 15 minutes:

3 cups thinly sliced onions

Turn into a large bowl and toss with:

4 cups mashed potatoes
½ to 1 cup dry unseasoned breadcrumbs
½ cup minced fresh parsley
2 teaspoons dried sage, or
    2 tablespoons minced fresh
½ teaspoon dried thyme, or
    1½ teaspoons minced fresh
Salt and ground black pepper to taste
1 large egg, lightly beaten
½ to 1 cup milk or Chicken Stock, 124, or a combination

Dot with:

2 tablespoons unsalted butter, cut into small pieces

Sprinkle with:

Grated Parmesan cheese

Use as a stuffing or turn into a large, shallow buttered baking dish and bake in a 350°F oven until browned and bubbly, 30 to 40 minutes.

Couscous Stuffing with Dried Apricots and Pistachios

About 4 cups

Best as stuffing for small, mild-flavored birds such as rock Cornish hens or poussins. For a sweeter stuffing, replace some of the apricots with finely diced dried dates.

Melt in a large saucepan over medium heat:

2 tablespoons unsalted butter

Add and cook, stirring, until tender, about 5 minutes:

½ cup finely chopped onions
½ cup finely diced carrots

Stir in and bring to a boil:

1½ cups Chicken Stock, 124
½ cup finely chopped dried apricots
1 tablespoon chopped preserved lemons (optional)
¼ teaspoon salt
¼ teaspoon ground black pepper
Pinch of ground cinnamon
Pinch of ground ginger

Stir in:

1 cup quick-cooking couscous

Remove from the heat, cover, and let stand for 5 minutes. Fluff with a fork and stir in:

½ cup chopped pistachios, whole pine nuts, or slivered blanched almonds, toasted
¼ cup minced fresh parsley

Use as a stuffing or serve immediately as a side dish.

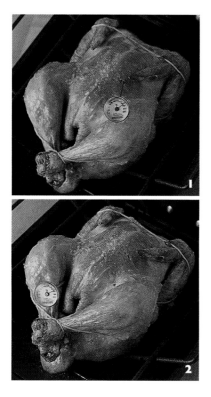

Testing for Doneness

The hard truth is that it is practically impossible to judge the doneness of a whole roasted bird without using an accurate instant-read thermometer.

To check the breast meat, insert the stem of the thermometer parallel to the breastbone deep into the neck end of the breast, where the meat is thickest (**1**). If the thermometer registers between 160° and 165°F, the breast meat is perfectly cooked, but that doesn't mean that the leg is done or that the stuffing, if there is one, has reached the safe temperature of 160°F. Test the stuffing as directed in *Rules for Stuffing Birds, 19*.

To check the leg, stick the stem of the thermometer into the thickest part of the thigh just beneath, but not touching, the bone, reaching all the way down to the joint (**2**).

If you like juicy, tender breast meat, consider the leg done at 170°F. At this temperature, the inside of the thigh, when pulled away from the body, will reveal a faintly ruddy glow, the meat will be on the firm side, and the leg joint will be slightly stiff and pinkish. If you find this unappealing, you can roast the bird until the leg reaches 175°F.

Those who do not like the slightest trace of pink in a bird should roast until the leg reaches 180°F. There is a drawback in doing this. The result of such thorough roasting is that the breast is inevitably overcooked.

RESTING BEFORE CARVING

Whole roasted birds must be allowed to rest outside the oven before carving so that the meat will become firm enough to slice neatly. For a chicken that has been roasted, a 10- to 15-minute rest is sufficient. For a rock Cornish hen, a 5-minute rest will do. Remove the bird from the roasting pan and place it on a plate deep enough to collect juices. It is important not to tent the bird with foil as the skin will become soggy. The roasted bird will release juices during resting. If you are making a sauce or gravy, be sure to add these delicious juices to it. Otherwise, you can spoon the juices over the carved meat or stir them into a vinaigrette for a salad served with the bird.

Carving a Roasted Chicken

Once the cooked bird has rested, remove the trussing twine. If the bird is stuffed, open the cavities, spoon the stuffing into a serving dish, and return it, covered, to the still-warm oven while you carve the bird as directed below and in *How to Carve a Roasted Chicken, opposite*.

The first task is to remove the legs. The hip joints of the chicken are such that this process is as easy as cutting along a dotted line. Having done so, the "oysters" are uncovered and can be removed one of two ways. If carving a small bird, whose thigh will be served whole, the oysters can be removed with the leg by making a lateral cut, toward the neck, before detaching the leg from the body. Follow the directions opposite to remove the oysters from larger birds.

Legs, of course, can be served whole, or can be split at the joint between the thigh and the drumstick. In order to do so, transfer the legs to a carving board and cut through the ball joint, separating the thigh and the drumstick.

You can remove the wings in one of two ways, both described opposite. In either case, you may choose to serve only meatier portions of the wings, saving the wing tips for stock.

There are two ways to carve the breast. Whichever method, it should be noted that thick slices of breast meat are less prone than thin slices to drying out and becoming cold.

HOW TO CARVE A ROASTED CHICKEN

1 Holding the bird in place with a large fork, cut through the skin where the leg is attached to the breast. Push the leg away from the body with the blade of the knife until the thighbone pops out of its socket. Cut down through the exposed thigh joint to remove the leg from the body. Repeat the process to remove the other leg.

2 The oysters, two nuggets of tender meat lodged on the back and attached to the thigh by skin, can be removed from a large bird by simply cutting off the leg, then tilting the carcass to one side and scraping the oyster free.

3 If you are carving a small chicken, cut into the breast about 1 inch up from the top of the wing joint, then cut down, scraping against the ribs, until you sever the joint. In this way, you will leave a small piece of breast meat attached to the wing, making a nice serving.

4 In the case of a large chicken, pry the wing away from the body with a fork until the joint is exposed, then cut through the joint.

5 You can carve the breast in one of two ways. Cut long, thin slices from one end to the other, parallel to the breastbone.

6 A more contemporary way to carve the breast is to remove an entire breast half from the bone, place it skin side up on a carving board, and cut crosswise on a diagonal into thickish slices.

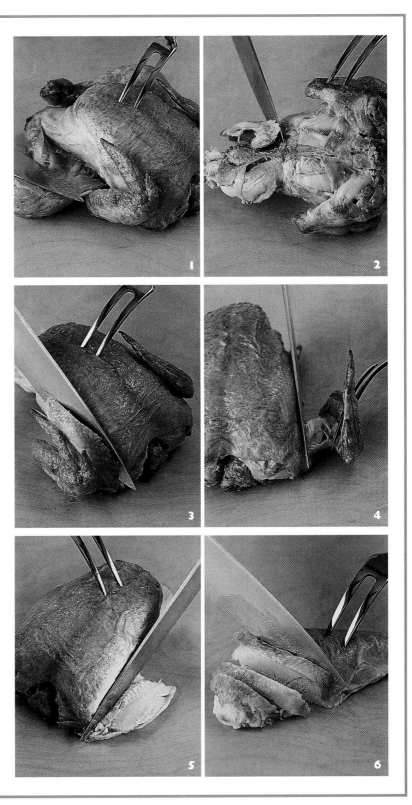

Roasted Chicken

4 to 7 servings; about 1 pound chicken per person

This is the simplest way of roasting a chicken. For the brownest skin, roast the bird on a rimmed baking sheet or in a shallow roasting pan.

Position a rack in the center of the oven. Preheat the oven to 400°F. Lightly oil a shallow roasting pan or baking sheet.

Remove the neck and giblets from, then rinse and pat dry:

1 whole chicken (4 to 7 pounds)

Generously rub the body and neck cavities and sprinkle the skin with:

Salt

Arrange the chicken breast side up in the pan. Brush the breast and legs with:

2 to 3 tablespoons melted butter

Put the chicken in the oven and roast. If you prize moist breast meat, consider the chicken done when the thickest part of the thigh exudes clear juices when pricked deeply with a fork and registers 170° to 175°F on an instant-read meat thermometer. If you like the dark meat

falling off the bone and are willing to risk a dry breast, roast until the thigh registers 180°F. The total roasting time for a 4-pound bird will be 55 to 65 minutes. For larger birds, figure 1 hour for the first 4 pounds, plus about 8 minutes for each additional pound. Remove the chicken to a platter and let stand for 10 to 15 minutes. Meanwhile, if you wish, make:

Poultry Pan Sauce or Gravy, opposite

Carve and serve.

Poultry Pan Sauce or Gravy

About 1 cup; 4 servings

These proportions are for a chicken weighing around 4 pounds. For a larger chicken or capon, double all ingredients. After removing the chicken to a platter, pour into the roasting pan:

¼ cup dry white wine, sherry, port, Madeira, or water

Place the roasting pan on two burners over medium-high heat. Bring the juices to a simmer and, using a wooden spoon, scrape up the browned bits on the bottom of the pan. Pour the mixture into a short drinking glass, let the fat rise to the top, skim off the fat with a spoon, and discard. (You can also use a gravy separator.) Return the mixture to the roasting pan or pour it into a small saucepan. Add the juices that have accumulated around the chicken along with:

¾ cup *Chicken Stock, 124*

Bring to a simmer. If you wish to thicken the sauce into a gravy, mix to a smooth paste:

1 tablespoon unsalted butter, softened

1 tablespoon all-purpose flour

Whisk the paste bit by bit into the simmering mixture and cook until thickened. Season with:

Several drops of fresh lemon juice or vinegar to taste

Salt and ground black pepper to taste

Turned Roasted Chicken

4 to 7 servings; about 1 pound chicken per person

This recipe calls for turning the chicken twice during cooking to ensure that the breast will still be tender and juicy by the time the dark meat is done.
Position a rack in the center of the oven. Preheat the oven to 400°F. Remove the neck and giblets from, then rinse and pat dry:

1 whole chicken (4 to 7 pounds)

Generously rub the body and neck cavities and sprinkle the skin with:

Salt

Set a V-rack or flat wire rack in a shallow roasting pan, place the chicken on the rack, and brush the skin all over with:

2 to 3 tablespoons melted butter

Position the chicken on its side, that is, with a leg facing up. If you are using a flat rack, you may need to prop the chicken up with balls of aluminum foil. Roast for 25 minutes for the first 4 pounds, plus 3 minutes more for each additional pound. Insert a wooden spoon or large metal spoon into the body cavity or grasp the chicken at both ends, with your hands protected with paper towels. Turn over on its other side, again propping with foil balls if necessary. Roast again for 25 minutes for the first 4 pounds, plus 3 minutes for each additional pound. Turn breast side up and roast 15 to 30 minutes more, until done. Remove the chicken to a platter and let stand for 10 to 15 minutes. Meanwhile, if you wish, make:

Poultry Pan Sauce or Gravy, above

Carve and serve.

Roasted Chicken and Vegetables

4 to 7 servings

Prepare the smaller amount of vegetables and other ingredients when roasting a 4- to 5-pound chicken, the larger amount when roasting a bigger bird. Since the vegetables should be cooked in a single jumbled layer, you will need to use a wide pan such as a 12 x 16 x ½-inch baking sheet. Because the vegetables will absorb most of the chicken drippings, it is not possible to make a pan sauce or gravy. Still, there will be a few browned bits on the bottom of the pan, which it will be worth your while to dissolve in a little chicken stock and pour over the chicken (opposite).

Position a rack in the center of the oven. Preheat the oven to 400°F.
Toss together to coat and combine:

Two to three 2- to 3-inch boiling potatoes, peeled and quartered
2 to 3 medium carrots, peeled, halved lengthwise, and cut into 1-inch pieces
Two to three 2-inch onions, peeled and quartered lengthwise
2 to 3 medium celery stalks, trimmed and cut into 1-inch pieces
2 to 3 tablespoons melted butter or vegetable oil
½ to ¾ teaspoon dried thyme
½ to ¾ teaspoon salt
Ground black pepper to taste

Remove the neck and giblets from, then rinse and pat dry:

1 whole chicken (4 to 7 pounds)
Generously rub the body and neck cavities and sprinkle the skin with:
Salt
Arrange in a roasting pan or on a rack in a roasting pan and brush with butter as directed for:
Roasted Chicken, 26, or Turned Roasted Chicken, 27
The vegetables need to cook for about 1 hour. If you are roasting a 4-pound chicken, scatter the vegetables over the roasting pan in a single layer as soon as the chicken goes into the oven. If you are roasting a larger chicken, add them to the pan about 1 hour before you estimate that the chicken will be done. (If the chicken happens to cook more quickly than you anticipate, continue to roast the vegetables while the chicken stands before carving.) Stir the vegetables every 15 to 20 minutes during cooking. Remove the vegetables to a platter and, if feasible, remove any fat in the pan. Pour into the pan:
⅓ to ½ cup Chicken Stock, 124
Set the pan on two burners over medium heat, bring the liquid to a simmer, and scrape with a spoon until the browned roasting bits are dissolved. Carve the chicken, arrange on the platter with the vegetables, and drizzle with the deglazing liquid.

Roasted Chicken with Herbs and Garlic

4 to 7 servings

Use these proportions for a chicken weighing 4½ pounds or less. Double the ingredients for a larger bird.
Position a rack in the center of the oven. Preheat the oven to 400°F.
Combine:

2 teaspoons minced fresh rosemary or thyme, or ¾ teaspoon dried, crumbled
1 teaspoon grated lemon zest (optional)
2 to 3 medium cloves garlic, minced
¼ teaspoon red pepper flakes
½ teaspoon salt

Remove the neck and giblets from, then rinse and pat dry:
1 whole chicken (4 to 7 pounds)
Generously rub the body and neck cavities and sprinkle the skin with:
Salt
Arrange in a roasting pan or on a rack in a roasting pan and brush with butter as directed for:
Roasted Chicken, 26, or Turned Roasted Chicken, 27
Using your fingers, loosen the skin and spread the herb mixture over the meat of the breast, thighs, and drumsticks. Roast as directed.

GARLIC

Fresh crops of garlic come to market from California in the summer months and from Mexico in the spring, but this member of the Onion (and thus of the Lily) family is available all year. When shopping for garlic, choose plump, firm heads of cloves with tight, papery skins that may be white, purplish, or tinged with red. Store away from light at room temperature. Avoid using cloves with brown spots or green sprouts—they are past their prime.

Roasted Stuffed Chicken or Capon

6 to 10 servings; about 1 pound chicken per person

When you want a festive stuffed bird, you should start with a chicken weighing 6 to 7 pounds or a capon. The cavities of smaller birds simply do not have enough space to accommodate a decent amount of stuffing. Capons weigh between 8 and 10 pounds. They may well be difficult to find, but a good butcher should carry them or be able to order one for you.

Position a rack in the center of the oven. Preheat the oven to 400°F.

Remove the neck and giblets from, then rinse and pat dry:

1 whole chicken (6 to 7 pounds), or 1 whole capon (8 to 10 pounds)

Generously rub the body and neck cavities and sprinkle the skin with:

Salt

Prepare and have hot:

1 recipe *Basic Bread Stuffing* or a variation, 20 and 22, or 1 recipe *Basic Corn Bread Stuffing* or a variation, 21

Loosely pack the stuffing into the body and neck cavities (see *Rules for Stuffing Birds*, 19). Sew or lace up the body cavity, sew the neck vent, or secure with small skewers or toothpicks. If you wish, perform a simple truss (see *How to Truss a Chicken*, 18). Roast as directed for *Roasted Chicken*, 26, or *Turned Roasted Chicken*, 27. The stuffing may increase the total roasting time by 10 to 20 minutes.

Roasted Rock Cornish Hens or Poussins

4 servings

Just like the rest of us, rock Cornish hens seem to put on a little weight with each passing year. If you can find hens in the 1¼- to 1½-pound weight range that used to be the norm, allow a whole bird per serving. Otherwise, buy two heavier hens and split each one to make two servings.

Position a rack in the center of the oven. Preheat the oven to 400°F. Lightly oil a baking sheet large enough to allow several inches of space between the birds. Remove the neck and giblets from, then rinse and pat dry:

4 small rock Cornish hens or poussins (under 1½ pounds), or 2 large rock Cornish hens (1¾ pounds or more)

Mix together, then rub into the body cavity and over the skin:

1½ teaspoons dried thyme

1 teaspoon salt

1 teaspoon ground black pepper

Arrange the birds breast side up on the pan. Brush the exposed skin with:

2 to 3 tablespoons melted butter

If you wish, place in each cavity:

1 small sprig fresh thyme or rosemary

Roast until the thickest part of the thigh exudes clear juices when pricked and registers 170° to 175°F on an instant-read thermometer, 25 to 30 minutes for small hens, 35 to 40 minutes for larger ones. (If you prefer your poultry very well done, roast a few minutes more, until the thigh registers 180°F. Remove the birds to a platter and let stand for 10 minutes. Meanwhile, if you wish, prepare:

Poultry Pan Sauce or Gravy, 27

If you have roasted larger birds, divide each one in half with a sharp knife or poultry shears before serving.

THYME

Rare is the poultry dish that cannot be enhanced by these tiny, pointed, gray-green leaves with their sweet wild-brush fragrance. There are several varieties of thyme available. Garden thyme is sometimes called English thyme. The French favor wild thyme for cooking, which, despite its name, is milder than garden thyme. Thyme is a hearty herb and is perfect for earthy dishes such as roasted game. Lemon thyme blends garden thyme's muted sweet flavor with clear lemon, a magnificent combination. Fresh thyme leaves and seeds have a good flavor after drying. Dried thyme should be packed in a tightly closed glass jar and kept in a cool, dark, dry place. (Keep in mind that glass best keeps aromas in—and out.) In a pinch, you could substitute young sage leaves and flowers in place of thyme.

Casserole-Roasted Chicken with Forty Cloves of Garlic

4 or 5 servings

Forty cloves may seem like a lot of garlic, but garlic loses much of its pungency and becomes nutty and sweet when roasted. Serve the unpeeled garlic cloves along with the chicken and let everyone have fun squeezing them out of their jackets.

Remove the neck and giblets from, then rinse and pat dry:

1 whole chicken (3½ to 4 pounds)

Rub the skin with:

Olive oil

Mix together, then rub into the body cavity and over the skin:

1 teaspoon dried thyme, crumbled

1 teaspoon dried sage, crumbled

½ teaspoon salt

½ teaspoon dried rosemary, crumbled

½ teaspoon ground black pepper

Place in the cavity:

1 lemon, quartered

If you wish, perform a simple truss (see *How to Truss a Chicken*, 18). Arrange the chicken breast side up in a casserole, cover, and refrigerate for 2 to 24 hours.

Position a rack in the center of the oven. Preheat the oven to 375°F. Add to the casserole with the chicken:

3 heads garlic, cloves separated but not peeled

1¼ cups Chicken Stock, 124

1 cup dry white wine

Bring to a boil, cover the casserole, and roast the chicken for 25 minutes. Increase the oven temperature to 450°F, uncover the casserole, and roast the chicken until the thigh exudes clear juices when pricked deeply with a fork and registers 170° to 175°F on an instant-read thermometer, 35 to 60 minutes

more. Check to make sure there is always some liquid in the bottom of the casserole; add a little more wine or stock if needed. Remove the chicken and garlic from the casserole and keep warm. Skim as much fat as possible from the pan juices with a spoon. If the pan juices are watery or weak in flavor, boil them down over high heat to concentrate. (Transfer the juices to a saucepan if your casserole cannot withstand direct heat.) If you wish, peel 6 or more of the garlic cloves, mash to a paste, stir into the sauce,

and boil for 1 minute. Remove the sauce from the heat and stir in, if you wish:

2 tablespoons minced parsley or finely shredded basil or 2 teaspoons minced fresh thyme, tarragon, or rosemary

Season with:

Salt and ground black pepper to taste

Cut the chicken into serving pieces and arrange on a platter. Spoon the pan juices over it and scatter the garlic cloves around it.

CASSEROLE ROASTING

Casserole roasting is a cooking method as much akin to braising as it is to roasting. Here, as in braising, the meat is cooked, covered, in a small amount of liquid. With the cooking vessel closed, the liquid, as well as the juices from the food, condenses on the lid and supplies a measure of continuous basting. When the casserole lid is removed from the cooking vessel, the food begins to roast. In the case of chicken, the skin will brown and crisp slightly, forming a wonderful golden case for the moist, tender meat inside.

Roasted Chicken Stuffed Under the Skin

4 servings

Position a rack in the center of the oven. Preheat the oven to 400°F. Remove the neck and giblets from, then rinse and pat dry:

1 whole chicken (about 3½ pounds) or 2 rock Cornish hens (at least 1½ pounds each)

Prepare:

Duxelles, right, or Spinach-Ricotta Stuffing, opposite

Butterfly the bird(s) (see *Butterflying or Splitting a Bird*, 13). Inserting your hand at the wing end of the breast, loosen the skin over the breast and around the thigh and drumstick. Generously pack the stuffing under the skin, first pushing it over the drumstick and thigh and then over the breast. Cut a ½-inch slit in the skin on either side of the breast, about 1 inch from the tip, and slip the end of 1 drumstick into each opening. Smooth the stuffing with your hands to give the bird(s) a plump but natural shape. Place the bird(s) skin side up on a rack in a shallow roasting pan.

Brush with:

1 to 2 tablespoons melted butter

Roast until the thickest part of the thigh exudes clear juices when pricked deeply with a fork and registers 170° to 175°F on an instant-read thermometer, 45 to 50 minutes for the chicken, 25 to 30 minutes for the hens.

PLACING STUFFING UNDER THE SKIN

Stuffing placed between the skin and breast meat of a bird flavors it and helps keep it moist while cooking. Fine-textured stuffings work best. They are easy to handle when stuffing and easy to carve through when cooking is done.

Easing in your hand at the neck end of the bird, loosen the skin over the breast and around the thigh and drumstick. Move as far down the breast as you can go without tearing the skin (**1**).

Pack the stuffing evenly down the length and across the width of the breast, wrapping the flap of the skin at the neck end of the bird over the stuffing (**2**).

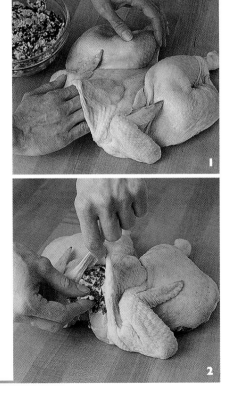

Duxelles

About ½ cup

Squeeze all the moisture out of the chopped mushrooms or they will not brown properly.

Chop very fine or pulse in a food processor until they resemble coarse sand:

8 ounces mushrooms, wiped clean

Squeeze about ¼ cup of the mushrooms at a time in dampened cheesecloth or a thin cotton towel and wring them very hard to extract their bitter juices. The mushrooms will be in a solid lump if you have squeezed hard enough. Heat in a medium skillet until the foam subsides:

1½ tablespoons butter
1 teaspoon vegetable oil

Add and cook briefly over medium heat:

2 tablespoons very finely minced shallots or scallions (white part only)

Add the mushrooms and cook, stirring often, over medium-high heat until they have begun to brown and there is very little liquid, 5 to 6 minutes. Stir in:

1 tablespoon dry sherry or Madeira

Cook until completely evaporated. Add:

¼ cup heavy cream (optional)
Salt and ground black pepper to taste
Pinch of dried thyme

Let cool, then refrigerate in a container for up to 10 days or freeze for up to 3 months.

Spinach-Ricotta Stuffing

About 2 cups

Stuff this mixture under the skins of chicken pieces or of a whole, butterflied, flattened bird, 13. If substituting frozen spinach, thaw a 10-ounce box of frozen spinach, squeeze it to remove excess liquid, chop coarsely, then toss with the breadcrumbs and ricotta cheese.

Heat in a large skillet or Dutch oven over medium-high heat until wilted:

One 12-ounce bunch or 10-ounce bag spinach, trimmed, washed, and coarsely chopped

Remove from the heat. When the spinach is cool enough to handle, squeeze out the excess liquid. Return the pan to medium heat and heat:

2 teaspoons olive oil

Add and cook, stirring, until tender, 3 to 4 minutes:

½ cup finely chopped onions

1 teaspoon minced garlic

Combine the spinach and sautéed vegetables in a large bowl and toss with:

1 cup ricotta cheese

½ cup soft breadcrumbs from day-old bread

2 tablespoons grated Parmesan cheese

2 teaspoons olive oil

½ teaspoon salt

¼ teaspoon ground black pepper

Pinch of freshly grated or ground nutmeg

Use as a stuffing.

ABOUT
BROILED
CHICKEN

For broiling, small chickens are wanted. Large chickens simply take too long to cook through; by the time they are done, the skin has charred and the kitchen has filled with smoke. In years past, a cook proposing to broil a chicken would buy a so-called broiler/fryer, that is, a small chicken weighing 2½ to 3 pounds. Today, alas, chickens in this weight range rarely appear at supermarkets, and the term broiler/fryer has lost its meaning, for it is often applied to chickens weighing as much as 4½ pounds.

To make the best of this imperfect situation, buy a 3½-pound chicken, or the smallest one you can find, and split it or divide it into parts yourself. If you must use chicken parts, buy the smallest ones available and examine the package to make sure that it does not contain an oversized leg or breast half. (The parts in a package do not necessarily come from the same chicken.) Another alternative is to broil rock Cornish hens. Split the hens, removing the backbones, and serve a half to each person.

Broiled Lemon Garlic Chicken, 37

Broiling Times

Broiling times in recipes are inevitably inexact because the broiling elements of home ranges vary greatly in the intensity of their heat. As a general rule, chicken should be placed 6 to 8 inches beneath the preheated element and broiled for 15 minutes on the bone side and then for 10 to 15 minutes on the skin side. (Always broil the bone side first, or the skin will become soggy.) When very hot broilers are used, however, it may be necessary to move the chicken much farther from the heat to prevent charring, and when the chicken is moved away from the heat, it may take somewhat longer to cook through.

Broiled Chicken or Rock Cornish Hens

4 servings

Preheat the broiler.

Rinse and pat dry:

**1 chicken (about 3½ pounds),
    2 rock Cornish hens (1½ to
    1¾ pounds), or 3½ pounds
    chicken parts**

If broiling a whole chicken or hens, cut the bird(s) in half, removing the backbone, and make a shallow incision on the inside of each leg at the drumstick/thigh joint to help the heat penetrate. Arrange the pieces skin side down on a broiler tray and brush the exposed side with:

**2 tablespoons melted butter or
    olive oil**

Sprinkle liberally with:

**Salt and ground black pepper
    to taste**

Place the pan 7 to 8 inches beneath the broiler element and broil 15 minutes for the chicken, 10 minutes for the hens, and 12 to 15 minutes for the chicken parts. Turn the pieces skin side up and brush with:

**1 to 2 tablespoons melted butter or
    olive oil**

Sprinkle with:

Salt and ground black pepper

Broil until the skin is browned and crisp and the thigh releases clear juices when pricked deeply with a fork, 15 to 20 minutes for the chicken, 6 to 8 minutes for the hens, and 8 to 10 minutes for the chicken parts. (If the skin begins to char before the cooking time is up, move the pan farther from the heat.) Remove the broiled pieces to a platter. If you wish, prepare:

Poultry Pan Sauce or Gravy, 27

To maximize the flavor of the sauce, slowly pour the wine (or water) and stock used to make the sauce over the broiling tray, still set over the bottom pan, all the while scraping the tray with a wooden spoon to dissolve the browned bits.

BROILING WITH RUBS, PASTES, AND MARINADES

Since barbecued and grilled chicken tastes divine when rubbed with herbs and spices or coated with a flavorful herb or spice paste, it would seem logical to treat broiled chicken in the same way. Unfortunately, things are not so simple. When you prepare chicken on an outdoor grill, you can prevent charring by moving the chicken away from the coals, damping the fire, or covering the grill rack. But the broiling elements of most indoor ranges have only one setting—high—and many gas ranges do not permit the cook to set the chicken lower than 8 inches from the broiling element. The inevitable result is that rubs and pastes burn. If you want to apply a rub or paste, you are better off baking the chicken and then crisping the skin under the broiler, if you wish (see *Baked Chicken with Chili-Garlic Spice Paste*, 42). Marinades, as well as glazes and sauces, tend to blacken and require special handling. Choose one that does not include sugar or a sweet ingredient such as molasses, honey, jelly, or jam. Any garlic in a marinade should be put through a garlic press or minced almost to a paste, or else it will leave unpleasant blackened bits on the chicken skin. Sauces and glazes, which often contain ingredients easily charred, must be applied separately to each side of the chicken shortly before that side is cooked through.

Always broil chicken in a two-piece broiling pan with a perforated broiling tray, which allows fat and dripping cooking juices to drain away and collect in the pan below. When chicken is broiled in a flat pan, the fat is directly exposed to the heat and will smoke and may even catch fire.

Broiled Lemon Garlic Chicken

4 servings

Combine in a large bowl:
¼ cup strained fresh lemon juice
¼ cup olive oil
**1 to 2 tablespoons pressed or very
 finely minced garlic**
1 tablespoon Dijon mustard
½ teaspoon dried thyme
1 teaspoon salt
1 teaspoon ground black pepper
Rinse, pat dry, and cut up the
chicken or hens as directed for:
**Broiled Chicken or Rock Cornish Hens,
 opposite**
Place the pieces in the bowl with
the marinade, turn to coat well,
and refrigerate, covered, for 1 to
3 hours. Broil, brushing with the

marinade instead of butter or oil
and omitting the salt and pepper.
Remove the broiled pieces to a platter. If you wish to make a pan sauce,
pour over the broiling tray (still set
over the broiling pan), all the while
scraping with a wooden spoon:
**½ cup dry white wine or Chicken
 Stock, 124**
Remove the broiling tray and skim
the fat off the juices in the broiling
pan with a spoon. Place the pan on
two burners over medium heat and
boil the juices until concentrated
and flavorful. Spoon the sauce over
the chicken and sprinkle with:
2 tablespoons minced fresh parsley

BROILED CHICKEN WITH BARBECUE SAUCE

*Applying the barbecue sauce shortly
before the chicken is finished cooking helps prevent the sauce from
burning. This dish (above) is traditional summer fare. Serve with slaw
and/or potato salad.*
Prepare *Broiled Chicken or
Rock Cornish Hens, opposite.*
About 2 minutes before the
chicken or hens are fully cooked,
brush both sides with about
1 cup *Barbecue Sauce, 120.*
Return to the broiler skin side up
and broil until the skin and sauce
have charred slightly and the flesh
is done. If the sauce threatens to
burn, move the pan farther from
the heat.

ABOUT
BAKED
CHICKEN

*T*he term "baked chicken" always implies a dish prepared with chicken parts. (A whole chicken, when baked, is said to be roasted.) Baking is certainly the easiest technique for cooking chicken parts and produces excellent results.

If you are lucky enough to be cooking for a crowd that unanimously prefers either white or dark meat, bake breasts or legs only. This way, you will not have to worry about the breasts drying out while the legs finish cooking. If you are preparing drumsticks and/or thighs only, you can bake them just until the juices run clear or, if you prefer, until the meat falls off the bones. Breasts, though, should be removed from the oven as soon as the flesh is no longer pink, or else the meat will be dry and tough.

Baked Chicken with Tomatoes, Ham, and Madeira, 41

Baked Chicken with Onions, Garlic, and Rosemary

4 to 5 servings

This simple but delicious dish is Greek in inspiration, so you might serve it in the Greek style with oven-roasted potatoes cooked with olive oil, garlic, and herbs.

Position a rack in the center of the oven. Preheat the oven to 400°F. Rinse and pat dry:

3½ to 4½ pounds chicken parts

Season liberally with:

Salt and ground black pepper to taste

Toss together:

3 medium onions, cut into rings
6 to 12 cloves garlic, thinly sliced
2 tablespoons olive oil

4 teaspoons minced fresh rosemary, or 2 teaspoons dried, crumbled

Spread half of the onion mixture in a shallow baking dish or roasting pan just large enough to hold the chicken pieces in a single layer. Arrange the chicken pieces skin side up on top, then cover with the remaining onion mixture. Drizzle over the chicken:

2 tablespoons olive oil

Bake the chicken until the dark meat pieces exude clear juices when pricked deeply with a fork, 45 to 55 minutes.

ROSEMARY

From a distance, rosemary's leaves appear like diminutive pine needles on long, thin branches. The leaves are gray-green to green and sharp. No leaves are more pungent. Their fragrance and flavor might be described as pine mixed with mint. This is not an herb that can be subtle. Because the leaves are tough, chop them fairly fine. This releases even more of their flavor. The leaves dry well. To substitute dried rosemary for fresh, use a generous ¼ teaspoon ground or 1 teaspoon crumbled dried leaves for every tablespoon of fresh rosemary finely chopped. Store fresh rosemary in the refrigerator. If necessary, you could use fresh oregano leaves, for their pungency, or sweet basil leaves and flowers in place of fresh rosemary.

Baked Chicken with Orange Juice

4 servings

A perfect quick after-work dinner. The ingredients can be readied in the time it takes the oven to preheat. For best effect, use a good-quality Dijon mustard and freshly squeezed orange juice.

Position a rack in the center of the oven. Preheat the oven to 375°F. Rinse and pat dry:

1 chicken (about 3 pounds), quartered, or 3 pounds chicken parts

Smear the skin with:

4 teaspoons Dijon mustard

Arrange the chicken skin side down in a shallow roasting pan or baking dish just large enough to hold it in a single layer. Sprinkle the pieces with:

½ cup finely chopped onions
2 tablespoons unsalted butter, cut into bits
Salt and ground black pepper to taste

Pour around the chicken:

1½ cups orange juice

Bake, basting once, for 30 minutes. Turn the chicken skin side up and sprinkle with:

¼ cup firmly packed dark brown sugar

Bake until the chicken is tender and golden, 15 to 20 minutes more. Add more orange juice if the pan seems dry. Remove the chicken to a serving platter. Pour the juices into a small saucepan and boil over high heat until syrupy. Spoon the sauce over the chicken and serve.

Baked Chicken with Tomatoes, Ham, and Madeira

4 to 5 servings

Position a rack in the center of the oven. Preheat the oven to 350°F. Rinse and pat dry:

3 to 4 pounds chicken parts

Season with:

Salt and ground black pepper to taste

Combine:

4 ounces smoked ham, diced
1 medium onion, thinly sliced
1 cup chopped seeded peeled tomatoes, fresh or canned
2 cloves garlic, chopped
1 tablespoon whole-grain mustard
½ cup Madeira or sweet sherry

¼ cup dry white wine
1 tablespoon olive oil
1 teaspoon dried marjoram or oregano
½ teaspoon salt
¼ teaspoon ground black pepper

Spread this mixture in the bottom of a shallow roasting pan or baking dish just large enough to hold the chicken in a single layer. Place the chicken pieces skin side up on top and brush lightly with:

Olive oil

Bake, uncovered, for 45 to 60 minutes, basting every 15 minutes with the pan juices and adding a little wine, water, or *Chicken Stock*, 124, if the pan seems dry. The chicken is done when the dark meat pieces exude clear, not pink, juices when pricked deeply with a fork. Remove the chicken to a platter. Tilt the roasting pan and skim as much fat as possible from the pan juices. Taste and adjust the seasonings, then pour the sauce over the chicken. If you wish, sprinkle the chicken with:

Grated Parmesan cheese
Chopped fresh parsley

HOW TO PEEL AND SEED TOMATOES

Here's the standard method for removing both skin and seeds.

1 Cut a small X in the bottom of the tomatoes—do not cut the flesh. Ease them into a pot of boiling water. Leave ripe tomatoes in for about 15 seconds, barely ripe tomatoes in for twice as long. Lift them out with a sieve and drop into a bowl of ice water to stop the cooking.

2 Pull off the skin with the tip of the knife. If the skin sticks, return the tomato to the boiling water for another 10 seconds and repeat. If the dish can use a touch of smoky flavor and if you have a gas burner, an easier way to peel tomatoes is to hold the tomato on a long-handled fork over the burner, turning it until the skin splits. Do not plunge in water, but after cooling, peel as above.

3 To seed and juice a tomato, cut it crosswise in half (between the top and bottom). Squeeze each half gently, cut side down, over a strainer set in a bowl to catch the juice, which you can add to the dish you're making. Now run the tip of a finger into each of the cavities and flick out the mass of seeds. Depending on the variety, tomatoes produce varying amounts of seeds and juice.

BAKED CHICKEN WITH ASIAN GINGER SPICE PASTE

Pungent and gingery.
Prepare *Baked Chicken with Chili-Garlic Spice Paste, right,* substituting 1 cup *Asian Ginger Spice Paste, 118,* for the chili paste.

BAKED CHICKEN WITH THAI GREEN CURRY PASTE

Fragrant and fiery.
Prepare *Baked Chicken with Chili-Garlic Spice Paste, right,* substituting 1 cup *Thai Green Curry Paste, 116,* for the chili paste.

Baked Chicken with Chili-Garlic Spice Paste

4 servings

A taste thrill for those who like their chicken highly seasoned. Serve with steamed jasmine rice.

Rinse and pat dry:

3½ to 4½ pounds chicken parts

Using about 2 tablespoons per piece, coat the chicken on all sides with:

1 cup Chili-Garlic Spice Paste, 118

Cover and refrigerate for 2 to 24 hours.

Position a rack in the center of the oven. Preheat the oven to 350°F. Lightly oil a shallow roasting pan. Arrange the chicken pieces skin side down in the pan. Bake for 20 minutes. Using tongs, turn the chicken skin side up and bake until the dark meat pieces exude clear juices when pricked deeply with a fork, about 20 minutes more. If you wish to crisp the skin, run the chicken briefly under a hot broiler.

Oven-Barbecued Chicken

4 servings

This recipe could not be easier.
Position a rack in the center of the oven. Preheat the oven to 350°F.
Rinse and pat dry:

3½ to 4½ pounds chicken parts
Season liberally with:

Salt and ground black pepper
Have ready:

1 cup *Barbecue Sauce*, 120
Place the chicken in a shallow roasting pan or baking dish, brush with two-thirds of the sauce, and arrange skin side down in a single layer. Bake for 20 minutes. Using tongs, turn the chicken skin side up. Paint with the remaining barbecue sauce and bake until the dark meat pieces exude clear juices when pricked deeply with a fork, about 20 minutes more. If you wish to crisp and color the skin, run the chicken briefly under a hot broiler.

Baked Mustard Chicken

4 servings

Perfect for an easy supper.
Position a rack in the center of the oven. Preheat the oven to 350°F.
Lightly oil a baking sheet.
Rinse and pat dry:

3½ to 4½ pounds chicken parts
Brush the chicken pieces liberally with:

About ⅓ cup Dijon mustard
Combine in a wide, shallow bowl:

2 cups dry unseasoned breadcrumbs
¼ cup minced fresh parsley
2 tablespoons unsalted butter, melted

2 cloves garlic, minced
1 teaspoon salt
½ teaspoon ground black pepper
Coat each piece of chicken with the crumb mixture, patting with your fingers to make the crumbs adhere. Place the chicken skin side up on the baking sheet. Bake until the coating is nicely browned and the dark meat pieces exude clear juices when pricked with a fork, 45 to 60 minutes. For a crispier crust, run the chicken briefly under a hot broiler. Serve immediately or at room temperature.

SUBSTITUTING DRIED HERBS FOR FRESH

Strengths in leaves vary, but the general rule is to use a generous ¼ teaspoon ground or 1 teaspoon crumbled dried leaves for every tablespoon of the fresh herbs finely chopped. Most fresh herbs are perishable. Store bunches in the refrigerator, their stems in water. Pack loose leaves and flowers in perforated plastic bags in the refrigerator crisper. If there is excess moisture in the leaves, pat them fairly dry, then crush a dry paper towel at the bottom of the bag and place the leaves on top. A little moisture helps keep them fresh, but too much promotes decay.

Deviled Boneless, Skinless Chicken Breasts

6 servings

In cooking, use of the word "deviled" traditionally signifies the use of red pepper. In this recipe, a marinade made with hot red pepper sauce gives ordinary chicken some kick.

Rinse, pat dry, and trim any excess fat from:

6 boneless, skinless chicken breast halves

If desired, remove the white tendon running through the tenderloins. Arrange the breasts in a baking dish large enough to hold them in one layer. Pour over the chicken breasts:

Soy and Sherry Marinade, 114

Roll the breasts until they are completely coated with marinade, then cover the dish and refrigerate for at least 2 hours or up to 12 hours, turning the chicken once or twice.

When ready to cook, position a rack in the center of the oven. Preheat the oven to 375°F. Mix together with a fork in a small bowl:

1 cup fresh breadcrumbs

2 tablespoons unsalted butter, melted

½ teaspoon ground black pepper

Drain and discard any excess marinade from the chicken, leaving the breasts in the dish. Cover the chicken evenly with the breadcrumb mixture and bake, uncovered, until the chicken and crumbs are browned and the chicken is firm when pressed, 20 to 30 minutes. Serve immediately.

Chicken Parmigiana

2 to 4 servings

The Italian-American classic that everyone loves. This dish can be assembled early in the day, refrigerated, and then baked when needed.

Prepare:

Breaded Chicken Cutlets, opposite

Position a rack in the center of the oven. Preheat the oven to 350°F. Lightly oil a 13 x 9-inch baking pan or shallow baking dish. Spoon into the pan:

½ cup Italian Tomato Sauce, opposite

Arrange the chicken cutlets over the sauce, slightly overlapping them. Sprinkle with:

3 to 4 tablespoons grated Parmesan cheese

Spoon over:

1 cup Italian Tomato Sauce, opposite

Top with:

6 ounces mozzarella cheese, thinly sliced

½ cup grated Parmesan cheese

Cover the pan with aluminum foil and bake until heated through, 20 to 30 minutes. If you wish to brown the top, remove the foil and run the dish briefly under a hot broiler. Serve hot, sprinkled with:

Chopped fresh parsley (optional)

PARMIGIANO-REGGIANO

This mouth-filling cow's milk cheese with a complex and pleasing aftertaste is made in a small, legally designated area of Emilia-Romagna in northern Italy. It is the only true Parmesan. All the others are imitations. Older is *not* better. Today's Parmigiano-Reggiano usually reaches its peak at about two years. Before World War II, when different cows gave Parmigiano-Reggiano milk, the cheese successfully aged longer. Surprisingly, an aged Monterey Jack cheese and a Wisconsin Asiago are closer in flavor than American and Argentinian Parmesans. Parmigiano-Reggiano is easily grated or shredded. Sometimes a small chunk of it is added to long simmered dishes to impart its mellow, nutty flavor.

Italian Tomato Sauce

Use fresh or canned tomatoes.
Heat in a large skillet over medium heat:

2 to 3 tablespoons extra-virgin olive oil

Add:

⅓ cup finely chopped fresh parsley
I medium onion, finely chopped
I small carrot, peeled and finely chopped
I celery stalk with leaves, finely chopped

Cook, stirring, until the onions are golden brown, about 5 minutes. Add:

2 cloves garlic, minced
½ cup packed fresh basil leaves, chopped, or I sprig each fresh rosemary, sage, and thyme

Cook, stirring, for about 30 seconds. Stir in:

2½ pounds ripe tomatoes, peeled, if desired, seeded, and coarsely chopped, or one 28-ounce can and one 14-ounce can whole tomatoes, with juice, crushed between your fingers as you add them to the pan
I tablespoon tomato paste (optional)
Salt and ground black pepper to taste

Simmer, uncovered, until the sauce is thickened, about 10 minutes. Remove the herb sprigs.

Breaded Chicken Cutlets

2 to 4 servings

This recipe forms the base for Chicken Parmigiana, opposite.
Rinse and pat dry:

4 boneless, skinless chicken breast halves (about I½ pounds)

Trim any fat around the edges. If you wish, remove the white tendon running through the tenderloins. Place the cutlets I at a time between sheets of wax paper and gently pound with a mallet or the side of an empty bottle to flatten slightly. Combine in a wide, shallow bowl:

I cup dry unseasoned breadcrumbs
¼ cup grated Parmesan cheese (optional)
I tablespoon minced fresh parsley or basil (optional)
I teaspoon salt
½ teaspoon ground black pepper

Whisk together in a shallow bowl:

I large egg
I teaspoon water

Spread on a plate:

¼ cup all-purpose flour

Coat the chicken with the flour and shake off the excess. Dip in the egg mixture and then coat with the breadcrumb mixture, patting with your fingers to make the crumbs adhere. Heat in a heavy 10- to 12-inch skillet over medium-high heat until shimmery and fragrant:

⅓ cup olive oil

Add the chicken and cook until lightly browned, 2 to 3 minutes. Using tongs, turn the cutlets and cook, 2 to 3 minutes more, adding a little more oil if the pan looks dry. Quickly blot the chicken with paper towels.

Southwestern Chicken Baked in Parchment

4 servings

This method of cooking, in French, en papillote, *results in moist and tender meat.*

Rinse and pat dry:

4 boneless, skinless chicken breast halves (about 1½ pounds)

Lay on a work surface with the smoother side up. Make an incision about 3 inches long and 2 inches deep in the middle of the thick side to create a pocket. In a small bowl, combine:

4 ounces mild goat cheese, at room temperature

2 medium fresh jalapeño peppers, seeded and minced

3 sun-dried tomato halves in oil, minced

Spoon one-quarter of the filling into each pocket. Press to seal the edges. Generously season each chicken breast with:

Salt and ground black pepper to taste

Refrigerate for at least 15 minutes. Meanwhile, combine:

2 cups cooked black beans (about ⅔ cup dried), rinsed and drained if canned

1 small red onion, finely chopped

⅓ cup chopped fresh cilantro

3 tablespoons olive oil

1 teaspoon ground cumin

1 teaspoon red wine vinegar

Pinch of ground red pepper

Preheat the oven to 375°F.

Cut four 15-inch squares of parchment paper and crease them in half on the diagonal. Spoon about ½ cup of the black bean mixture on one side of each piece of parchment; top with a chicken breast and sprinkle with:

Hot paprika

Fold the empty half of the parchment paper over the chicken to cover. Fold the edges of the parchment together all the way around, closing the packet tightly. Set on baking sheets and bake until the packets are browned and puffed, about 25 minutes. Serve with:

Lime wedges

COOKING BLACK BEANS

From Mexico to Cuba to Brazil, black beans, also called turtle beans, signify the rich flavors of Latin American cooking. They are often called *frijoles negros*, "black beans" in Spanish. They have a wonderful earthiness that stands up to lots of onions and garlic, chili peppers, and spices. Medium sized, with a white dot along one edge, they hold their black color in cooking and color the liquid too.

Black beans are thin skinned and, therefore, cook quickly. To cook, simmer soaked or unsoaked beans in water, covered, for 30 to 60 minutes. If you would like to soak the beans before cooking, pour boiling water over the beans to cover by 2 inches. Cover and let stand until the beans have swelled to at least twice their size and have absorbed most of the water, about 1 hour. Drain the beans and cook as directed above.

Chicken Breasts Baked on Mushroom Caps

4 to 6 servings

For the most attractive presentation, use the caps of portobello, shiitake, or large button mushrooms.

Position a rack in the center of the oven. Preheat the oven to 400°F. Rinse, pat dry, and trim any excess fat from:

6 bone-in or boneless chicken breast halves (with skin)

Season with:

1 teaspoon dried thyme
Salt and ground black pepper to taste

Lightly oil a 13 x 9-inch baking pan or shallow baking dish just large enough to hold the chicken pieces in a single layer. Remove the stems from:

6 large portobello mushrooms or 12 to 18 large shiitake or button mushrooms, wiped clean

Or cut into ¼-inch-thick slices:

Enough smaller mushrooms to cover the bottom of the pan

Arrange the mushrooms, gill side down and overlapping if necessary, in the pan. Sprinkle with:

1 tablespoon minced garlic
Salt and ground black pepper to taste

Pour over the mushrooms:

2 cups dry white wine

Lay the chicken breasts skin side up on top of the mushrooms. Brush lightly with:

Olive oil

Bake, uncovered, until the chicken skin turns golden brown, about 20 minutes. Check to see that there is some liquid in the pan; if not, add more wine. Baste the chicken with pan juices and turn the pieces over. Bake until the chicken is firm and

fully cooked, 10 to 20 minutes more. Using a slotted spoon, remove the chicken and mushrooms to a platter, arranging the chicken skin side up on the mushrooms. Pour the pan juices into a small saucepan and skim the fat off the top with a spoon. For a low-fat sauce, add:

Enough water or *Chicken Stock*, 124, to measure 1 cup

For a more luxurious sauce, add:

½ to 1 cup heavy cream

Boil the sauce over high heat until reduced to a syrupy consistency. Taste and adjust the seasonings. Spoon some of the sauce over the chicken and pass the rest separately. If you wish, sprinkle the chicken with:

2 tablespoons minced fresh parsley

Boneless, Skinless Chicken Breasts Baked in Foil with Sun-Dried Tomatoes and Olives

4 servings

Sun-dried tomatoes and Kalamata olives make a gutsy garnish for boneless, skinless chicken breasts (opposite). Position a rack in the center of the oven. Preheat the oven to 450°F. Rinse and pat dry:

4 boneless, skinless chicken breast halves (about 1½ pounds)

Trim any fat around the edges. If you wish, remove the white tendon running through the tenderloins. Season with:

Salt and ground black pepper to taste

Combine:

10 Kalamata or other black olives, pitted and finely chopped

8 sun-dried tomato halves in oil, cut into thin strips

3 tablespoons sun-dried tomato oil (from the jar of tomatoes) and/or olive oil

2 tablespoons finely shredded fresh basil or minced fresh parsley

Cut four 12-inch squares of aluminum foil. Fold each square in half to make a crease at the center. Unfold the foil and lightly oil the shiny side. Lay each breast on the shiny side of the foil just to one side of the crease. Spoon the tomato mixture over each breast, leaving a ¼-inch border around the edges. Loosely fold the foil over the chicken, then crimp the edges of the packet to seal tightly. Place the packets on a baking sheet and bake for 20 minutes. Remove from the oven and let stand for 5 minutes. To avoid being burned by steam, cut a slit in the packets before opening them.

Baked Stuffed Boneless Chicken Breasts

6 to 8 servings

This recipe can be prepared using boned, split chicken breasts without the skin or with the skin still attached. The skin becomes brown and crisp and keeps the delicate meat moist. Position a rack in the center of the oven. Preheat the oven to 350°F. Rinse and pat dry:

8 boneless chicken breast halves (about 3 pounds), with or without the skin

Trim any fat around the edges. If you wish, remove the white tendon running through the tenderloins. Place the chicken breasts 1 at a time between sheets of wax paper and gently pound with a mallet or the side of an empty bottle until about ⅜ inch thick. Season with:

Salt and ground black pepper to taste

Heat in a small skillet over medium-high heat until the foam begins to subside:

2 to 3 tablespoons unsalted butter

Add and cook, stirring, until tender but not brown, about 5 minutes:

⅓ cup finely chopped onions

Stir in and cook for 30 seconds:

1 teaspoon minced garlic

Remove the mixture to a bowl and stir in:

2 cups dry unseasoned breadcrumbs

¼ cup grated Parmesan cheese

¼ cup finely chopped fresh parsley

½ teaspoon dried rosemary, crumbled

½ teaspoon dried sage, crumbled

½ teaspoon salt

½ teaspoon ground black pepper

Stir in:

⅓ to ⅔ cup *Chicken Stock*, 124

The stuffing should be just moist enough to hold together in a crumbly ball when squeezed firmly in the hand. Do not overmoisten. Taste and adjust the seasonings.

Lightly oil a 13 x 9-inch baking pan. Place ¼ cup stuffing on the center of the underside of each breast and press lightly to compact it. Bring the top and bottom flaps of the chicken up over the stuffing, slightly overlapping the ends, then fold up the sides to enclose the stuffing completely. Lay the packets seam side down in the pan and brush with:

Olive oil

Season with:

Salt and ground black pepper to taste

Bake until the chicken is lightly browned and feels firm when pressed, 20 to 30 minutes. Serve immediately.

Chicken Pot Pie

6 to 8 servings

You can use your favorite rolled or drop biscuit dough or Flaky Pastry Dough *to make the crust. The* Creamed Chicken *is a standard filling.*

Prepare, using ½ cup flour:

Creamed Chicken, opposite

Prepare the dough for:

1 recipe *Flaky Pastry Dough*, opposite

Position a rack in the upper third of the oven. Preheat the oven to 400°F. Butter a 13 x 9-inch baking pan or other shallow baking dish.

Heat in a large skillet over medium-high heat until the foam begins to subside:

2 tablespoons unsalted butter

Add and cook, stirring often, until barely tender, about 5 minutes:

1 medium onion, chopped

**3 medium carrots, peeled and
  sliced ¼ inch thick**

**2 small celery stalks, sliced
  ¼ inch thick**

Stir the vegetables into the creamed chicken along with:

¾ cup frozen peas, thawed

3 tablespoons minced fresh parsley

Pour the chicken mixture into the prepared pan. If using a rolled biscuit dough, cut the dough into biscuits and arrange on top of the chicken, overlapping the biscuits if necessary. If using a drop biscuit recipe, simply drop small biscuits on top. If using pie dough, roll it out into the shape of the pan, place on top of the chicken, and tuck the edges in against the pan sides. For a golden brown glaze, brush the top with:

2 tablespoons beaten egg (½ large)

Bake until the chicken is bubbly and the topping is nicely browned, 25 to 35 minutes.

Creamed Chicken

This recipe includes directions for poaching raw chicken. It is the filling used for Chicken Pot Pie, opposite.

3½ pounds chicken parts or 1½ pounds boneless, skinless chicken breast

Place the chicken in a Dutch oven. Add:

1¾ to 2 cups *Chicken Stock, 124*

Pour in just enough water to cover the pieces. Chicken parts may require as much as 3 cups water to be covered, while boneless, skinless breasts may not need any at all. Bring to a simmer over high heat, then reduce the heat so that the poaching liquid barely bubbles. Partially cover and cook until the meat releases clear juices when pierced with a fork, 25 to 30 minutes for chicken parts, 8 to 12 minutes for boneless, skinless chicken breast. Remove the meat from the stock and let stand until cool enough to handle. If using chicken parts, remove and discard the skin and bones. Cut or shred the meat into bite-sized pieces. Skim the fat from the stock with a spoon. Melt in a large saucepan over medium-low heat:

4 tablespoons (½ stick) unsalted butter

Add and whisk until smooth:

⅓ cup all-purpose flour (for a creamed dish), or ½ cup (for a pot pie or casserole)

Cook, whisking constantly, for 1 minute. Remove the pan from the heat. Add 2 cups of the chicken stock and whisk until smooth. Whisk in:

1½ cups whole milk, half-and-half, or light cream

Increase the heat to medium and bring the mixture just to a simmer, whisking constantly. Remove the pan from the heat, scrape the inside of the saucepan with a wooden spoon or heatproof rubber spatula, and whisk vigorously to break up any lumps. Return the pan to the heat and, whisking, bring to a simmer and cook for 1 minute. Stir in the cooked chicken along with:

2 to 3 tablespoons sherry (optional)

Cook for 1 minute more. Remove from the heat and season to taste with:

Several drops of lemon juice

Salt and ground white or black pepper

2 to 3 pinches of freshly grated or ground nutmeg

Flaky Pastry Dough

One 9-inch pie crust

Using a rubber spatula, thoroughly mix in a large bowl:

1¼ cups all-purpose flour

½ teaspoon white sugar or 1½ teaspoons powdered sugar

½ teaspoon salt

Add:

½ cup solid vegetable shortening, or ¼ cup shortening and 4 tablespoons (½ stick) cold unsalted butter

Break the shortening into large chunks; if using butter, cut it into small pieces, then add it to the flour mixture. Cut the fat into the dry ingredients by chopping vigorously with a pastry blender or by cutting in opposite directions with 2 knives, one held in each hand. As you work, periodically stir dry flour up from the bottom of the bowl and scrape clinging fat off the pastry blender or knives. When you are through, some of the fat should remain in pea-sized pieces; the rest should be reduced to the consistency of coarse crumbs or cornmeal. The mixture should seem dry and powdery and not pasty or greasy. Drizzle over the flour and fat mixture:

3 tablespoons ice water

Using the rubber spatula, cut with the blade side until the mixture looks evenly moistened and begins to form small balls. Press down on the dough with the flat side of the spatula. If the balls of dough stick together, you have added enough water; if they do not, drizzle over the top:

1 tablespoon ice water

Cut in the water, again using the blade of the spatula, then press with your hands until the dough coheres. The dough should look rough, not smooth. Press the dough into a round flat disk, and wrap tightly in plastic. Refrigerate for at least 30 minutes, and preferably for several hours, or for up to 2 days before rolling. The dough can also be wrapped airtight and frozen for up to 6 months; thaw completely before rolling.

ABOUT
SAUTEED
& STIR-FRIED CHICKEN

*S*auter *literally means "to jump," and if the French did not invent the technique, they certainly taught us the nuances. The cooking is done in a small amount of hot fat in an open shallow pan and works well for chicken, especially those cuts that cook quickly. The pan and the fat in it must be hot enough that, when the chicken is added, it sears it at once, preventing sticking.*

Stir-frying, one of the basic methods of Chinese cooking, is another excellent match for quick-cooking chicken parts and pieces. It involves three essential elements: the use of very high heat for a brief cooking time; using just enough peanut oil to cook the dish well; and the cutting of all the ingredients to a more or less similar size so that they cook in about the same amount of time. If the cooking time of ingredients is very different although they have been cut to approximately the same size, they may be cooked separately and then combined all at once at the end. In every case, stir-frying involves flipping and stirring the ingredients very rapidly in a wok or skillet.

Stir-Fried Garlic Chicken, 62

Sautéing

Food cut to a uniform thickness and size sautés best. To ensure a dry surface, food for sautéing is frequently floured or breaded. If cold, it will reduce the heat. If wet, it will not brown properly. Steam will also form if the pan is crowded; there must be space between the pieces of food you are sautéing. Boneless, skinless chicken breasts are ideal for sautéing.

For most sautés use a combination of butter and oil. When the fat becomes very fragrant (but not smoking), it is time to start (**1**). With chicken breasts, the handsomest side goes into the pan first (**2**); that first sizzle browning usually is not duplicated when the food is turned. Generally, chicken is cooked through when the juices rise to the surface of the cooked side. If breaded pieces fail to brown, turn up the heat and, if necessary, add more fat to the pan. During cooking you may need to reduce the heat on the second side.

To serve sautéed chicken with a simple sauce, remove the chicken from the pan and keep it warm on a hot serving dish. Quickly deglaze the delicious residue on the bottom of the pan with stock or wine (**3**). Reduce the liquid into a sauce, season, and pour over the sautéed chicken.

Stir-Frying

In classic stir-frying, all the ingredients are always bite-sized, the stirring is ceaseless, and the heat is extremely high. In fact, on some home stoves it is hard to get the heat high enough.

Familiarize yourself with the recipe, since you may not have time to stop and read once you are in action. You will want to allow yourself plenty of preparation time, since cutting food into small pieces to cook rapidly can be time-consuming. Have all ingredients within easy reach of the stove. Paying attention to cooking time is critical as food cut into small pieces cooks quickly. Undercook

rather than overcook—you can always return food to the heat.

On gas burners, either a round- or a flat-bottomed wok will work; for all other burners, a flat-bottomed wok is preferable. A 12- to 14-inch wok is ideal, but you can stir-fry beautifully in a skillet as long as it is heavy and large—the largest your burner will accommodate. The pan and surface must be capable of being heated empty over the highest heat without damage. Always heat the empty wok (or skillet) until it just begins to smoke, then add the oil and tip the wok to coat it before proceeding with the recipe.

Sautéed Boneless, Skinless Chicken Breasts

2 to 4 servings

Sautéed chicken breasts should be a rich nut-brown on the outside, tender and veritably bursting with juice inside. The secret to success is high heat—not so high as to burn the fat, but pretty close. At low heat, the chicken simply dries out and turns to leather. If the pan is hot enough, the chicken will take— more or less exactly—4 minutes per side to cook through. Sautéed boneless, skinless chicken breasts are delicious on their own but even better when served with a simple sauce made in the pan, 27. An onion conserve or tangy salsa would also be good served alongside.

Rinse and pat dry:

4 boneless, skinless chicken breast halves (about 1½ pounds)

Trim any fat around the edges. If you wish, remove the white tendon running through the tenderloins. Sprinkle both sides with:

Salt and ground black pepper to taste

Spread on a plate:

¼ cup all-purpose flour

Coat the chicken on both sides with the flour, pressing to make the tenderloins, the thin strips of meat on the undersides of the breasts, adhere. Gently shake off the excess flour, holding the chicken tapered side up to avoid detaching the tenderloins. Heat in a heavy 10- to 12-inch skillet over medium-high heat until fragrant and nut-brown:

1½ tablespoons unsalted butter

Add:

1½ tablespoons olive oil

Swirl the butter and oil together. Arrange the chicken tenderloin side down in the skillet and sauté for exactly 4 minutes, keeping the fat as hot as possible without letting it burn. Using tongs, turn the chicken and cook until the flesh feels firm to the touch and milky juices appear around the tenderloins, 3 to 5 minutes more. Serve immediately, or remove to a platter and keep warm in a very low oven while you prepare a sauce for the chicken.

Chicken Cordon Bleu

2 to 4 servings

This classic has never lost its appeal.

Rinse and pat dry:

4 boneless, skinless chicken breast halves (about 1½ pounds)

Trim any fat around the edges. If you wish, remove the white tendon running through the tenderloins. Place the chicken breasts 1 at a time between sheets of wax paper and gently pound with a mallet or the side of an empty bottle until about ⅜ inch thick. Season with:

Salt and ground black pepper to taste

Cover half of the underside of each chicken breast with:

1 thin slice ham or prosciutto

Leaving a small space around the edges, top the ham slice with:

1 thin slice Gruyère or other Swiss cheese

Fold the chicken breast in half over the ham and cheese and press the edges firmly to seal. Make a ⅛-inch cut along the folded edge of the breast to help prevent the packet from opening during cooking. Combine in a wide, shallow bowl:

1 cup dry unseasoned breadcrumbs

¼ cup minced fresh parsley

1 teaspoon salt

½ teaspoon ground black pepper

Whisk together in a shallow bowl:

1 large egg

1 teaspoon water

Spread on a plate:

¼ cup all-purpose flour

Working 1 at a time, press both sides of each packet in the flour, then dip in the egg mixture and coat with the breadcrumb mixture, patting with your fingers to make the crumbs adhere. Heat in a heavy 10- to 12-inch skillet over medium-high heat until fragrant and nut-brown:

1½ tablespoons unsalted butter

Add:

1½ tablespoons olive oil

Swirl the butter and oil together. Place the packets in the skillet and cook, until nicely browned, 3 to 4 minutes. Using tongs or a spatula, turn the packets and cook for 3 to 4 minutes more. Drain on paper towels and serve immediately.

Sautéed Boneless, Skinless Chicken Breasts Piccata

2 to 4 servings

Prepare and keep warm in a 200°F oven:

Sautéed Boneless, Skinless Chicken Breasts, opposite

Remove all but about 1 tablespoon of the fat in the skillet, heat over medium heat, and add:

2 to 3 tablespoons minced shallots or scallions

Cook, stirring, until wilted, about 1 minute. Increase the heat to high and add:

1 cup Chicken Stock, 124

Bring to a boil, scraping the bottom of the skillet with a wooden spoon to dissolve the browned bits. Add:

3 to 4 tablespoons strained fresh lemon juice

2 tablespoons nonpareil capers, drained

Boil until the mixture is reduced to about ⅓ cup, 3 to 4 minutes. Add any accumulated chicken juices and reduce again. Remove from the heat and swirl in:

2 to 3 tablespoons unsalted butter, softened

Pour the sauce over the chicken and serve immediately.

Sautéed Boneless, Skinless Chicken Breasts with Sherried Mushroom Cream Sauce

2 to 4 servings

Prepare and keep warm in a 200°F oven:

Sautéed Boneless, Skinless Chicken Breasts, opposite

Remove all but about 2 tablespoons of the fat in the skillet, heat over medium heat, and add:

2 to 3 tablespoons minced shallots or scallions

Cook, stirring, until wilted, about 1 minute. Increase the heat to high and add:

8 ounces mushrooms, thinly sliced (about 2⅓ cups)

Cook, stirring, until the mushrooms are softened and lightly browned, 2 to 3 minutes. Add:

⅓ cup sweet or dry sherry

Boil until the sherry is nearly evaporated, about 1 minute. Add:

1 cup heavy cream

½ cup Chicken Stock, 124

Boil until the sauce is thick enough to lightly coat a spoon, about 5 minutes. Add any accumulated chicken juices and reduce again until thick. Stir in:

2 tablespoons finely chopped fresh parsley

Pinch of freshly grated nutmeg

Salt and ground white or black pepper to taste

Season with:

Several drops of fresh lemon juice

Spoon the sauce over the chicken and serve immediately.

CAPERS

These are the preserved buds of a white flower on a spiny Mediterranean shrub. Freshly picked, the buds are startlingly bitter, reminiscent of raw artichoke hearts. Once cured in salt or brine, their flavor mellows without losing its citruslike tartness. The smallest caper buds are called nonpareil. Large, fully formed caper berries, with their stems still attached, are also available and are quite dramatic in appearance, especially when used as a garnish in gin and vodka martinis. The one essential ingredient in tapenade is the caper—*tapeno* in Provençal. Capers are far better packed under salt but are usually found in brine. Always drain and rinse capers before using, however they are packed. Chopped gherkins can be used instead of capers in some dishes.

Sautéed Boneless, Skinless Chicken Breasts with Tomatoes, Capers, and Basil

2 to 4 servings

Prepare and keep warm in a 200°F oven:

Sautéed Boneless, Skinless Chicken Breasts, 56

Remove all but about 2 tablespoons of the fat in the skillet, heat over medium heat, and add:

⅓ cup minced shallots or scallions

Cook, stirring, until the shallots are softened, about 1 minute. Increase the heat to high and add:

¼ cup dry white wine or vermouth

Boil, scraping the bottom of the skillet with a wooden spoon, until the wine is almost evaporated. Stir in:

1 pound tomatoes, seeded and chopped (about 2 cups)

2 tablespoons nonpareil capers, drained

1 tablespoon minced garlic

Cook, stirring constantly, until the tomatoes have given up their juice, creating a thick chunky puree, about 2 minutes. Add any accumulated chicken juices and boil the sauce until thick.

Remove from the heat, and stir in:

2 tablespoons finely shredded fresh basil

Salt and ground black pepper to taste

Spoon the sauce over the chicken (opposite) and serve immediately.

Sautéed Boneless, Skinless Chicken Breasts with Balsamic Citrus Sauce

2 to 4 servings

Prepare and keep warm in a 200°F oven:

Sautéed Boneless, Skinless Chicken Breasts, 56

Remove all but about 1 tablespoon of the fat in the skillet, heat over medium heat, and add:

3 to 4 tablespoons minced shallots or scallions

1 heaping tablespoon honey

Pinch of ground allspice

Cook, stirring, until the shallots are wilted, 1 to 2 minutes. Increase the heat to high and add:

1 cup Chicken Stock, 124

1 tablespoon strained fresh lemon juice

Boil, scraping the bottom of the skillet with a wooden spoon, until reduced to about ½ cup. Add:

¼ cup heavy cream

Boil until the sauce is slightly thickened, about 1 minute. Add:

1 tablespoon balsamic vinegar

Salt and ground black pepper to taste

Return to a boil, then spoon the sauce over the chicken and serve immediately.

BALSAMIC VINEGARS

Balsamic vinegars fall into two categories: artisan and commercial. Traditional, artisan-made balsamics, the more expensive of the two, are far more liqueur than salad dressing and are made only in the provinces of Modena and Reggio in northern Italy's Emilia-Romagna region. Boiled-down grape must concentrates over years of passing through a series of wooden barrels stored carefully in airy attics. By law artisan balsamic contains no wine vinegar. This balsamic is aged 12 years for "*vecchio*" (old), and 25 years for "extra *vecchio*." Its guarantee of authenticity is the word *tradizionale* on its label. Use traditional balsamic as an intense sauce, by the drop, on finished dishes.

Commercial balsamic can be produced anywhere and is usually wine vinegar with caramel added to it. Better examples have some boiled-down must. Quality ranges from poor to fine, as no regulations govern its production. Use commercial balsamic in marinades, in dressings, and cooked into recipes.

Chicken Kiev

4 to 8 servings

This justly famed entrée consists of thinly pounded boneless, skinless chicken breasts that are rolled around fingers of seasoned butter, breaded, and sautéed. The key to success in preparing this dish is to seal the chicken packets tightly and to bread them with care so that the butter does not leak out during cooking.

Using the back of a wooden spoon, cream together in a medium bowl:

½ pound (2 sticks) unsalted butter, softened

2 tablespoons strained fresh lemon juice

1 tablespoon minced fresh parsley

1 tablespoon finely snipped fresh chives, or 2 teaspoons dried (optional)

1 teaspoon minced garlic

½ teaspoon salt

¼ teaspoon ground black pepper

On a sheet of wax paper, shape the butter into a 6 x 3-inch cake and refrigerate for 2 hours.

Rinse and pat dry:

8 boneless, skinless chicken breast halves (about 3 pounds)

Trim any fat around the edges. If you wish, remove the white tendon running through the tenderloins. Place the breasts 1 at a time between sheets of wax paper and gently pound with a mallet or the side of an empty bottle until ¼ inch thick. Season with:

Salt and ground black pepper to taste

Divide the chilled butter crosswise into 8 fingers, each 3 inches long. Arrange the chicken tender side up on a work surface. Place 1 finger of butter crosswise on each breast about one-third of the way up from the tapered end. Fold the tapered end over the butter, then roll the butter up inside the remainder of the breast, tucking in the sides to enclose the butter completely.

Combine in a wide, shallow bowl:

2 cups dry unseasoned breadcrumbs

1 teaspoon salt

1 teaspoon ground black pepper

Whisk together in a shallow bowl:

2 large eggs

2 teaspoons water

Spread on a plate:

½ cup all-purpose flour

Coat the chicken packets in the flour, being sure to cover the tucked-in ends. Roll the packets in the egg mixture, then coat on all sides with the breadcrumb mixture, patting with your fingers to make the crumbs adhere. Place the rolls on a rack, cover loosely with wax or parchment paper, and refrigerate for 1 to 8 hours.

Position a rack in the center of the oven. Preheat the oven to 350°F. Heat in a skillet large enough to hold the rolls in a single layer over medium-high heat until shimmery:

½ cup vegetable oil

Arrange the rolls in the skillet and cook until the first side is nut-brown, 2 to 3 minutes. Turn carefully with a slotted spatula and brown the second side in the same manner. Using the spatula, transfer the rolls to a baking sheet and bake for 15 minutes. Serve immediately.

SHAPING CHICKEN KIEV

Place 1 finger of butter crosswise on a breast half about one-third of the way up from the tapered end. Fold the tapered end over the butter (**1**), then roll the butter up inside the remainder of the breast.

Continue rolling and tuck in the sides to enclose the butter completely (**2**).

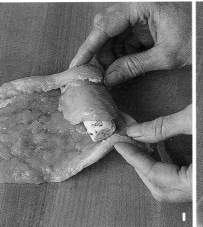

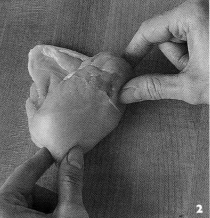

Stir-Fried Garlic Chicken

2 to 4 servings

BEFORE COOKING:

In a medium bowl, mix together thoroughly:

1 tablespoon cornstarch
1 tablespoon Chinese cooking wine or dry white wine
2 teaspoons light soy sauce
2 teaspoons oyster sauce
1 teaspoon salt
1 teaspoon sugar

Cut into 1½ x ½-inch pieces:

1½ pounds boneless, skinless chicken thighs

Toss in the soy sauce mixture. Cover with plastic wrap and let stand for 20 to 30 minutes. On a small plate, place:

4 teaspoons finely minced garlic
1 tablespoon finely minced peeled fresh ginger

On another small plate, place:

20 snow pea pods, trimmed
1 medium onion, cut into ¼-inch-thick slices

In a small bowl, mix together thoroughly:

1 tablespoon hoisin sauce
1 tablespoon ketchup
1 tablespoon toasted sesame oil
1½ teaspoons dark soy sauce
½ teaspoon red pepper flakes

Have ready:

⅔ cup *Chicken Stock*, 124
3 scallions, sliced lengthwise into thin strips, then cut into 2-inch sections

TO COOK:

Heat a wok or large skillet over high heat until hot.

Add:

2 tablespoons peanut oil

Swirl the oil around the pan until very hot but not smoking. Add the minced garlic and ginger and stir briefly until the garlic is very slightly browned. Add the chicken and quickly stir and flip in the oil to separate the pieces. Continue to toss and cook for about 3 minutes. Add the chicken stock and swirl until the stock is heated through. Add the snow peas and onions, stir once, cover, and cook for 2 minutes. Uncover the pan and add the soy sauce mixture. Stir lightly until all pieces are thoroughly coated. Sprinkle with the scallions, stir lightly, and remove to a serving dish. Serve immediately.

Stir-Fried Ginger Chicken

4 servings

BEFORE COOKING:

In a medium bowl, mix together thoroughly:

1 egg white, lightly beaten
1½ tablespoons cornstarch
½ teaspoon salt

Cut into ¾-inch cubes:

3 boneless, skinless chicken breast halves

Toss in the egg white mixture. Let stand for 20 to 30 minutes.

Place on a small plate:

3 scallions, cut into ¼-inch pieces
2 tablespoons finely minced peeled fresh ginger

In a medium bowl, mix together thoroughly:

2 tablespoons plus 2 teaspoons sugar
½ teaspoon salt
2 tablespoons ketchup
4 teaspoons white vinegar
4 teaspoons Chinese cooking wine or dry white wine
2 teaspoons dark soy sauce

In a cup, mix together thoroughly, leaving the spoon in for later:

2 teaspoons cornstarch
2 teaspoons cool water

TO COOK:

Heat a wok or large skillet over high heat until hot. Add:

½ cup peanut oil

Swirl the oil around the pan until very hot but not smoking. Add the chicken and quickly stir and flip in the oil to separate the pieces. Cook lightly. Remove with a slotted spoon, leaving the oil in the wok or skillet. Set aside.

Reheat the wok or skillet over high heat. Swirl the remaining oil around the pan until it is very hot but not smoking. Add the scallions and ginger. Stir and toss vigorously until slightly brown, about 30 seconds. Add the soy sauce mixture and stir until heated through. Stir the cornstarch mixture, then pour it slowly into the sauce, stirring constantly. Cook, stirring until the mixture is thickened. Return the chicken to the wok or skillet. Cook, stirring thoroughly to mix, until heated through. Remove to a serving dish. Serve immediately.

Asian Seasonings

HOISIN SAUCE

This brownish red member of the soybean family is almost always sweet, garlicky, and spicy. It has the anise flavor of five-spice powder and is peppered with a little dried chili. The texture ranges from a creamy jam to a runny sauce. Store for up to 1 year in a dark cupboard away from heat.

OYSTER SAUCE

Originally made from oysters, water, and salt only, oyster sauce now contains added cornstarch and caramel color, to improve its appearance and also to thicken liquids in stir-fries. When buying oyster sauce, avoid the cheaper varieties, which contain fewer oysters and more cornstarch. You can store it in the refrigerator for years.

PEANUT OIL

Peanut oil varies greatly in quality. When it has not been cold pressed (and most domestic peanut oil has not been), there is little or no peanut flavor. At Asian markets, you can find cold-pressed oils with a true peanut taste.

RICE WINE

Shaoxing (Shaoshing) is China's most famous rice wine (right). It comes from Shaoshing in Zhejiang province and has been made, it is said, for over 2,000 years. Blended glutinous rice, rice millet, a special yeast, and local mineral and spring waters give this amber-colored beverage its unique flavor. More like sherry in color, bouquet, and alcohol content (18 percent) than like sake or a grape wine, it is aged about ten years in earthenware and in underground cellars. The finest varieties age a century or more. Like sake, Shaoshing is drunk warm and is rarely left out of a dish; it is vital to Chinese cooking. A top-quality dry sherry is a good substitute.

Sake is the stronger Japanese version of rice wine—any brand of sake is suitable for use in cooking except those labeled "cooking wine," which are made from inferior rice wines and may contain additives. Sake also acts as a tenderizer in marinades and removes strong odors in cooking. When looking for a substitute, try pale dry sherry or dry vermouth.

SESAME OIL

In China, sesame oil is considered too expensive to cook with, but it is highly prized as a seasoning sprinkled over dishes just at the end of cooking. The best and most flavorful sesame oil is pressed from seeds that have first been toasted; oil made from raw seeds cannot compare in flavor. In Japan, tempura oil may contain up to one-half sesame oil and is suitable for deep-frying; sesame oil on its own burns too quickly to stand up to this kind of heat. It is best bought in glass bottles or tins, in which it goes rancid much less quickly than in plastic. Keep for only a month or two in a cool cabinet.

SOY SAUCE

Soy sauce is a naturally fermented product made in several steps and aged up to two years. Typically, roasted soybean meal and a lightly ground grain, usually wheat, are mixed with an *Aspergillis* mold starter; the resulting culture takes a few days to grow. Brine is then added to the fermented meal, along with a *Lactobacillus* starter and yeast. The mash is then aged slowly. When the producer determines that it is ready, the soy sauce is then strained and bottled. The Chinese invented soy sauce, and the Japanese learned the technology from them. The Chinese use both light and dark soy sauces. The latter is aged longer and toward the end of the processing is mixed with bead molasses, which gives it a dark caramel hue. Think of them as red and white wine, since as a rule, dark soy sauce flavors (and colors) heartier dishes, particularly those with red meat, whereas light soy sauce is used with seafood, vegetables, soups, and in dipping sauces.

ABOUT **BRAISED** CHICKEN

*T*he world's cuisines boast a wealth of fricassees, stews, and ragouts made with chicken. Definitions of these dishes overlap, but all involve braising chicken in liquid. After cooking, the liquid becomes a flavorful sauce or gravy, which can be thickened with flour or egg yolks or enriched with cream. Many of these dishes were originally made with hens past their egg-laying prime, whose tough, stringy flesh required slow braising in order to become tender. Today, with hens in short supply at the supermarket, most cooks choose ordinary young chickens instead.

Braising is perhaps the easiest and most forgiving of all cooking methods for chicken. Most people consider roasted, broiled, fried, or sautéed chicken disappointing when the white meat has been cooked to the point of becoming firm and dry. But they are happy with a thoroughly cooked braised chicken breast, because the sauce or gravy with which the chicken is served succeeds in masking the meat's dryness.

Chicken Étouffée, 68

Chicken Fricassee

4 or 5 servings

This delicate and creamy dish of chicken and vegetables has long been an American favorite.

Rinse and pat dry:

3½ to 4½ pounds chicken parts

Separate the legs into thighs and drumsticks; cut each breast half diagonally in half through the bone. If you wish, remove the skin. Sprinkle the chicken with:

Salt and ground black or white pepper to taste

Heat in a heavy 8- to 10-inch skillet over medium heat until fragrant and golden:

4 tablespoons (½ stick) unsalted butter

Place as many chicken pieces in the pan as will fit comfortably and cook, turning once, until pale golden, 3 to 5 minutes on each side. Remove the chicken to a plate and brown the remaining pieces in the same man-

ner. Add to the fat in the pan:

1½ cups chopped onions

Cook, stirring occasionally, until the onions are tender but not browned, about 5 minutes. Stir in:

⅓ cup all-purpose flour

Cook, stirring, for 1 minute, then remove the pan from the heat and whisk in:

2 cups hot water

1¾ cups *Chicken Stock*, 124

Whisking constantly, bring the mixture to a boil over high heat. Add:

8 ounces mushrooms, sliced (2⅓ cups)

3 medium carrots, peeled and diced (1 cup)

2 large or 3 medium celery stalks, diced (1 cup)

½ teaspoon dried thyme

1 teaspoon salt

½ teaspoon ground black or white pepper

Return the chicken pieces with all accumulated juices to the pan and bring to a simmer. Reduce the heat so that the liquid barely bubbles. Cover tightly and cook until the dark meat pieces exude clear juices when pricked with a fork, 20 to 30 minutes. Skim off the fat from around the sides of the pan with a spoon. If you wish, stir in:

¼ to ½ cup heavy cream

Season to taste with:

Salt and ground white or black pepper

Several drops of fresh lemon juice

The sooner the chicken is served, the juicier it will be. However, the dish can be made ahead. To serve within 1 hour, simply cover the pot and slide to a warm corner of the stove. Otherwise, let the chicken cool to tepid, then cover and refrigerate for up to 3 days.

Chicken and Dumplings

4 or 5 servings

This is another American favorite. These easy-to-make dumplings are the richest and fluffiest we know.

Prepare:

Chicken Fricassee, opposite

About 20 minutes before the chicken is done cooking, prepare the dumplings. Mix together:

2 cups all-purpose flour
1 tablespoon baking powder

¾ teaspoon salt

Bring just to a simmer in a small saucepan:

3 tablespoons butter
1 cup milk

Add to the dry ingredients. Stir with a fork or knead by hand 2 to 3 times until the mixture just comes together. Divide the dough into about 18 puffy dumplings. Roll each piece of dough into a rough ball. Degrease the pan juices and season the fricassee. Push the chicken pieces down so that they are submerged in gravy and gently lay the formed dumplings on the surface of the fricassee, cover, and simmer for 10 minutes. Serve immediately.

Cornmeal Dumplings

4 to 6 servings

These dumplings can also be used in Chicken and Dumplings *(above) or you can simmer and serve them in chicken stock.*

About 30 minutes before the chicken is done cooking, prepare the dumplings. Sift together:

¾ cup all-purpose flour
½ cup cornmeal
2 teaspoons baking powder
½ teaspoon salt

Cut in with a fork or pastry blender:

1 tablespoon cold butter

Whisk together:

1 large egg
⅓ cup milk

Stir into the dry ingredients just until blended. Gently drop teaspoonfuls of the batter onto the surface of the fricassee, cover, and simmer about 20 minutes.

DUMPLINGS

Simple, satisfying, and a particular treat in cold-weather months, dumplings take many forms. The English word *dumpling* originally meant something that was hollow. This idea of the dumpling still survives today in desserts such as apple dumplings, which consist of pastry or biscuit crusts wrapped around whole apples. Modern savory dumplings, however, are solid, made with a base of flour or cooked potatoes. There are two principal types. European dumplings such as potato gnocchi, spätzle, and *nockerln* are similar to fresh pasta in taste and texture. Although these dumplings are sometimes cooked in a soup or stew, they are more commonly simmered in water and then added to a dish or combined with butter or a sauce after they have been fully cooked. Most American dumplings, by contrast, are light, fluffy, and dry, akin to biscuits or cake. They are cooked on top of a stew, pot pie, or casserole and served directly out of the dish.

When cooking dumplings of either type, be sure to start with plenty of liquid, as dumplings absorb a lot. The liquid should be simmering—but not boiling—when the dumplings are dropped in, and kept at a simmer throughout cooking. Otherwise, the dumplings may become soggy or even disintegrate. You can usually cook European-style dumplings in advance and then add them to a hot soup or stew just before serving. To prevent the dumplings from turning soft and sticky, drain them well, lightly coat them with oil or melted butter, and store them in a single layer, covered, in the refrigerator for up to 2 days. It is important to remember that American-style dumplings must be served as soon as they are done, or they will become heavy.

Chicken Étouffée

4 to 6 servings

This is the classic Cajun way of making chicken fricassee. To give this dish its characteristic dark color and deep flavor, brown the chicken pieces thoroughly and cook the roux until nearly as dark as chocolate.

Rinse and pat dry:

4 to 5 pounds chicken parts

Mix together:

1 teaspoon paprika
1 teaspoon dried thyme
1 teaspoon salt
½ teaspoon ground black pepper
½ teaspoon dried basil
¼ teaspoon ground red pepper

Rub the spice mixture all over the chicken pieces. Pour into a doubled brown paper bag:

1 cup all-purpose flour

Shake 4 pieces chicken at a time in the bag to coat with flour; remove and shake off the excess. Repeat until all the chicken is coated. Reserve the flour. Heat in a wide, heavy skillet over medium-high heat until shimmery:

3 tablespoons vegetable oil

Add as many pieces of chicken to the skillet as will fit without crowding and brown on both sides to the color of dark toast, about 5 minutes each side. Remove the chicken, brown the remaining pieces in the same manner, and then remove them from the skillet as well. Remove all but about 3 tablespoons of the fat in the skillet. Reduce the heat to medium. Using a wooden spoon, stir in 3 tablespoons of the reserved flour. Cook, stirring constantly, until the roux is almost as dark as milk chocolate. This may take as long as 20 minutes. Stir in:

1 cup chopped onions
½ cup chopped celery
¼ cup chopped red bell peppers
¼ cup chopped green bell peppers
¼ cup chopped andouille sausage
**   or smoked ham**

Cook, stirring, until the vegetables are golden brown, 5 to 6 minutes. The roux will continue to darken to a deep mahogany color. Add:

2 tablespoons chopped garlic
¼ teaspoon dried sage, crumbled
¼ teaspoon dried thyme

Stir well and cook for 1 minute more. Stir in:

2 cups Chicken Stock, 124
3 tablespoons tomato paste
1 tablespoon Worcestershire sauce
¼ teaspoon hot red pepper sauce,
**   or to taste**

Stirring constantly, bring the sauce to a simmer. Return the chicken pieces with all accumulated juices to the skillet and bring the liquid back to a simmer. Reduce the heat so that the sauce bubbles gently. Cover the pan and cook, turning the pieces occasionally, until the chicken exudes clear juices when pierced with a fork, about 30 minutes. Remove the chicken to a plate. Skim the fat from the sauce with a spoon. Add:

½ cup finely chopped scallions
¼ cup chopped fresh parsley

Boil until the sauce is thickened. Season the sauce generously with:

Salt and ground black pepper
**   to taste**
Hot red pepper sauce

Return the chicken to the pan and heat through. Serve with:

Hot cooked rice

MAKING A ROUX

A roux is a mixture of fat and flour, cooked together, usually in equal amounts. Although exact amounts of fat and flour are called for in recipes, it is solely the amount of flour that determines the thickness of the sauce. Fat lubricates and smooths the flour so it does not form lumps when combined with stock or other liquid. The preferred fat is butter, but it could also be chicken or other poultry fat, rendered meat drippings, oil, or margarine.

A roux is started by melting butter or other fat, adding flour, and cooking the two together over low heat, whisking or stirring constantly to prevent scorching. During this process, which takes only a few minutes, the starch in the flour expands as it blends with the fat; if a roux cooks too quickly, the resulting mixture will be grainy. (If the fat floats to the top, the roux has separated; this happens rarely, but if it does, there is nothing to do but to throw out the roux and start over.)

There are three types of roux—white, blond, and brown, each with a different cooking time. White roux, used to make traditional white sauce, should be cooked just until the butter and flour are evenly incorporated and smooth and should be removed from the heat before the roux begins to darken at all, 3 to 5 minutes (**1**). Blond roux, used in velouté-based sauces and cream soups, cooks for a little longer, until it begins to give off a faint nutty aroma and turns an ivory color, 6 to 7 minutes (**2**). Brown roux, basic to Cajun and Creole cooking, cooks the longest—8 to 15 minutes and sometimes longer—until it is a dark brown and has a strong nutty fragrance (**3**). (The longer you cook a roux, the less it will thicken. The heat eventually breaks down the starch in the flour.)

Whether making white, blond, or brown roux, let it cool slightly before slowly whisking in the stock or other liquid. If you have made the roux in advance, it is important to first warm either it or the liquid to be added to it. Despite the legendary rule to add hot liquid to cold roux and cold liquid to hot roux, almost any combination will work. Simply avoid trying to combine cold roux and cold liquid, which would become lumpy, or hot roux and hot liquid, which would spatter. Once the roux and liquid are combined, stir constantly until the sauce is thickened and comes to a simmer. Once it has thickened, stir and skim often during the slow, gentle cooking needed to reduce the sauce to the desired consistency. Any trace of a floury taste will disappear after 10 minutes of slow simmering. If lumps do appear, strain the sauce through a fine-mesh sieve before proceeding.

The pan in which you make a roux should be chosen carefully. In an effort to prevent scorching, use a saucepan or skillet with a heavy bottom. Some cooks prefer enamel-covered cast iron, and others, cast iron au naturel.

Chicken Cacciatore

4 servings

Cacciatore *means "hunter's style" in Italian, and there are countless versions of this dish. Italian hunters who cook always seem to have tomatoes and olives handy. Flavors blossom when this dish is cooked a day ahead, just be sure to undercook slightly and reheat slowly to finish cooking. Rabbit can also be used in this dish. The flavor and aroma produced by the simple combination of its basic ingredients—chicken or rabbit, tomatoes, onions, herbs, red wine, and sometimes mushrooms— must not be missed. Polenta is a traditional companion.*

Rinse and pat dry:

3½ to 4½ pounds chicken parts

Season with:

Salt and ground black pepper to taste

Heat in a large, heavy skillet over medium-high heat until shimmery and fragrant:

3 tablespoons olive oil

Add the chicken pieces in small batches and brown on all sides; remove them to a plate as they are done. Remove all but 2 tablespoons of the fat in the pan. Reduce the heat to medium and add:

1 cup chopped onions

1 bay leaf

1½ teaspoons chopped fresh rosemary, or ½ teaspoon dried, crumbled

1 teaspoon minced fresh sage leaves, or ½ teaspoon dried, crumbled

Cook, stirring, until the onions are golden brown, about 5 minutes. Add:

1 large clove garlic, minced

Cook about 30 seconds more, being careful not to brown the garlic. Return the chicken to the skillet and pour in:

½ cup dry red or white wine

Cook over medium-high heat until all the wine is evaporated, turning the chicken and scraping up the browned bits on the bottom with a wooden spoon. Add:

8 ounces canned whole tomatoes, with juice, crushed with your hands

¾ cup Chicken Stock, 124

Reduce the heat to low, cover, and simmer gently for 25 minutes. Add:

½ cup oil-cured black olives, pitted and sliced (optional)

8 ounces mushrooms, sliced

Cook, covered, for 10 minutes. Uncover the pan and boil the pan juices over high heat until slightly thickened. Taste and adjust the seasonings. Serve with:

Soft Polenta with Butter and Cheese, below

Soft Polenta with Butter and Cheese

About 4 cups; 4 servings

This is the basic formula for stirred soft polenta. For more flavor, replace up to half of the water with chicken stock. Melt in a large saucepan over medium heat:

3 tablespoons butter

Add and cook, stirring, until translucent, about 5 minutes:

½ cup finely chopped onions

Stir in and bring to a boil:

3 cups water

Stir together:

1 cup water

1 cup yellow cornmeal

Gradually stir into the boiling water, reduce the heat to low, and cook, stirring constantly with a wooden spoon, until the cornmeal is very thick and leaves the side of the pan as it is stirred, about 25 minutes. Sprinkle with:

2 tablespoons to ½ cup grated Parmesan cheese

1 teaspoon salt, or to taste

Country Captain

4 servings

Versions of this fragrant, subtly sweet chicken curry have been prepared in American kitchens since colonial times.

Rinse and pat dry:

3½ to 4½ pounds chicken parts

Separate the legs into thighs and drumsticks; cut each breast half diagonally in half through the bone. Coat the chicken pieces on all sides with:

⅔ cup all-purpose flour

Heat in a wide, heavy pan over medium-high heat until fragrant and golden:

3 tablespoons unsalted butter

Add as many chicken pieces to the pan as will fit without crowding and brown to a deep golden color on both sides, 3 to 4 minutes each side. Remove the chicken to a plate and brown the remaining pieces in the same manner. When all the chicken has been browned and removed, add to the fat and cook until tender and golden around the edges:

2 cups chopped onions
1 large green bell pepper, diced

Stir in:

1 tablespoon curry powder
1 teaspoon ground ginger
½ teaspoon ground cinnamon
¼ teaspoon ground cloves
**¼ teaspoon freshly grated or
  ground nutmeg**

Cook slowly, stirring, for 1 minute. Add:

**One 14- to 16-ounce can whole
  tomatoes, with juice**
⅔ cup Chicken Stock, 124
⅔ cup dried currants or raisins
**3 tablespoons strained fresh lemon
  juice**
**1 tablespoon packed dark brown
  sugar**
2 to 3 cloves garlic, minced
½ teaspoon dried thyme
½ teaspoon salt
¼ teaspoon ground black pepper

Using a wooden spoon, lightly mash the tomatoes against the sides of the pan and scrape the bottom to dissolve the browned bits. Return the chicken to the pan and bring the liquid to a simmer over high heat. Reduce the heat so that the liquid barely bubbles. Cover tightly and cook, turning the pieces occasionally, until the chicken exudes clear juices when pricked deeply with a fork, 20 to 30 minutes. Remove the chicken to a plate. Skim the fat from the pan gravy with a spoon; if the gravy seems watery, boil it down over high heat. Return the chicken to the pan and heat through.

Serve with:

Hot cooked rice

CURRY

The word *curry* refers either to the aromatic leaves of the south Indian kari plant (curry leaves) or to a stew flavored with a blend of fragrant spices, often a premixed curry powder. Most American cooks are surprised to learn that a curry does not exist in traditional Indian cooking. The word is a British corruption of another Indian dish: perhaps of *kahri*, a Tamil word meaning sauce; or of *karhi*, a soupy north Indian dish of yogurt, which is thickened with chickpea flour; or of *kari*, a south Indian technique of stir-frying vegetables.

Basque Chicken

4 servings

Rinse and pat dry:

3½ to 4 pounds chicken parts

Heat in a wide, heavy Dutch oven over medium-high heat until fragrant:

3 tablespoons olive oil

Lightly brown the chicken in 2 batches in the hot oil, removing the browned chicken to a plate. Remove all but 3 tablespoons of the fat in the pan. Return the chicken to the pan and add:

2 pounds red and/or yellow bell peppers, cut into ½-inch strips

4 small fresh jalapeño peppers, seeded and minced

Four 2-ounce slices ham, cut into ½-inch squares

¼ cup chopped garlic (about 12 cloves)

¾ teaspoon salt

½ teaspoon ground black pepper

Place the pan over low to medium heat, cover tightly, and cook at a quiet sizzle, stirring often, until the chicken is cooked through and the peppers are soft, about 45 minutes. Meanwhile, prepare the sauce. Heat in a large saucepan over medium-high heat until fragrant:

2 tablespoons olive oil

Add:

2 to 3 cups chopped onions

Cook, stirring often, until the onions are tender but not browned, about 7 minutes. Add:

2 pounds fresh tomatoes, peeled, seeded, and chopped, or one 28-ounce can whole tomatoes, with juice, seeded and crushed

½ teaspoon salt

½ teaspoon ground black pepper

Bring to a boil, then reduce the heat to medium. Simmer, stirring often, until the sauce has thickened, about 20 minutes. Skim off any excess fat from the chicken with a spoon. Season both the chicken and sauce with:

Salt and ground black pepper to taste

Spoon onto a serving platter or divide among 4 plates:

4 to 6 cups cooked white rice

Arrange the chicken and pepper mixture over the rice. Serve immediately.

Coq au Vin

4 servings

When the old rooster, or coq, lost his crow, he would find himself the main ingredient in this classic French country fricassee. This dish is most commonly made with red wine, but white wine also can be used. If you would like to try a white, choose one that is flavorful and fruity, such as Riesling or Chardonnay.

Rinse and pat dry:

3½ to 4½ pounds chicken parts

Season with:

Salt and ground black pepper to taste

Cut into sticks ¼ inch wide:

4 ounces thick-cut bacon

Fry the bacon in a large, heavy Dutch oven over medium-high heat until it is nicely browned and most of its fat is rendered. Remove the bacon to a plate. Add as many pieces of chicken to the pan as will fit without crowding and brown until deep golden on both sides, about 7 minutes. Remove the chicken pieces and brown the remaining pieces in the same manner. Remove all but about 3 tablespoons of the fat in the pan. Add:

1 cup chopped onions

½ cup chopped peeled carrots

Cook, stirring occasionally, until the vegetables are tender, about 10 minutes. Stir in:

3 tablespoons all-purpose flour

Reduce the heat to low. Cook, stirring constantly, until the roux just begins to turn light brown, about 5 minutes. Stir in:

3 cups dry red wine

1 cup *Chicken Stock*, 124

2 tablespoons tomato paste

2 bay leaves

½ teaspoon dried thyme

½ teaspoon dried marjoram or oregano, crumbled

Increase the heat to high and bring the sauce to a boil, stirring constantly. Return the bacon and chicken with any accumulated juices to the pan. Return the sauce to a boil, then reduce the heat so that the liquid barely simmers. Cover and cook until the chicken exudes clear juices when pricked with a fork, 25 to 35 minutes. Meanwhile, measure:

1 to 2 cups pearl onions

Cut a tiny slice from both ends of each onion. Cover with boiling water and let stand for 1 minute.

Drain in a sieve, rinse with cold water, and pinch off the skins. Heat in a wide skillet over medium-high heat until fragrant and golden:

2 to 3 tablespoons unsalted butter

Add the onions and cook, stirring often, until they are lightly browned and just tender, 5 to 8 minutes. Add:

8 ounces mushrooms, sliced

Cook, tossing, until the mushrooms give up their juices. Remove from the heat. Remove the cooked chicken to a platter and cover with aluminum foil to keep warm. Bring the sauce to a boil over high heat and reduce until syrupy, using a spoon to skim off the fat as it accumulates. Add the onions and mushrooms with all juices to the sauce and heat through. Season with:

Salt and ground black pepper to taste

Pour the sauce over the chicken. If you wish, sprinkle with:

2 to 3 tablespoons minced fresh parsley

Serve with:

Boiled potatoes or noodles

Chicken Paprikash (Paprikás Csirke)

4 servings

This rich and delicious dish requires genuine Hungarian paprika. Sweet paprika is what you want, though you can add a little hot if you like spice.
Rinse and pat dry:

3½ to 4½ pounds chicken parts
Season generously with:

Salt and ground black pepper to taste

Heat in a wide, heavy skillet over medium-high heat until fragrant:

2 tablespoons butter or lard

Add as many pieces of chicken to the skillet as will fit without crowding and cook until golden on both sides, about 5 minutes. Remove the chicken to a plate and brown the remaining chicken in the same manner. Add to the fat remaining in the skillet:

3 cups very thinly sliced onions
Reduce the heat slightly. Cook, stirring, until the onions just begin to color, about 10 minutes. Sprinkle over the onions:

¼ cup sweet Hungarian paprika
2 tablespoons all-purpose flour
Cook, stirring, for 1 minute. Stir in:

1½ cups *Chicken Stock,* 124
1 tablespoon minced garlic
1 large bay leaf
½ teaspoon salt
½ teaspoon ground black pepper
Bring the mixture to a boil, stirring constantly. Return the chicken with all accumulated juices to the skillet. Reduce the heat so that the liquid barely bubbles, cover the skillet, and cook, turning the chicken once or twice, until the dark meat pieces

release clear juices when pricked with a fork, 20 to 30 minutes. Remove the chicken to a plate. Discard the bay leaf. Let the sauce settle, then skim the fat off the surface with a spoon. Boil the sauce over high heat until very thick, almost pasty. Remove the skillet from the heat and blend thoroughly into the sauce:

1 to 1½ cups sour cream
Return the sauce to high heat and boil until thickened. Season to taste with:

Salt and ground black pepper
Several drops of fresh lemon juice
Return the chicken to the skillet and heat through. Serve with:

Hot cooked noodles or *Spätzle,* opposite

Spätzle

4 or 5 servings

Spätzle, spätzen, or, more plainly, German egg dumplings are often served alongside a goulash or stew and are particularly welcome next to Chicken Paprikash, opposite. *Substituting milk for the water produces a richer, if slightly denser, dumpling. Spätzle are also delicious when pan-seared in a buttered skillet until the edges are crisp.*

Combine:

1½ cups all-purpose flour
½ teaspoon baking powder
¾ teaspoon salt
Pinch of freshly grated or ground nutmeg

Beat together:

2 large eggs
½ cup milk or water

Add to the flour mixture. Beat well with a wooden spoon to create a fairly elastic batter. Bring to a simmer in a large saucepan:

6 cups salted water

Drop small bits of the batter from a spoon into the bubbling liquid, or force the batter through a spätzle machine or colander to produce strands of dough that will puff into irregular shapes. Spätzle are done when they float to the surface. They should be delicate and light, although slightly chewy. If the first few taste heavy and dense, add a few more drops of milk or water to the batter before continuing. Lift the cooked spätzle from the saucepan with a strainer or slotted spoon. Serve spätzle as a side dish, sprinkled with:

Melted butter

Or melt in a small skillet over medium heat:

1 tablespoon butter

Add and cook, stirring, until toasted, 3 to 5 minutes:

⅓ cup fresh breadcrumbs

Sprinkle over the hot spätzle.

PAPRIKA

Finely ground dried ripe peppers constitute this spice. The color varies from light orange to deep red, the flavor from bland to rich but mild. *Sweet* paprika is ground from the flesh of particularly sweet peppers with most, if not all, of their seeds and ribs removed—these parts can be sharp tasting. By contrast, *hot* paprika is prepared with peppers whose flesh contains more heat; some seeds and ribs may be added. Most paprikas are blends that fall between sweet and hot. The best paprika has long come from Hungary, where paprika making is an important culinary tradition. Once opened, Hungarian paprika must be stored tightly closed in the refrigerator or, even better, in the freezer to maintain freshness. If need be, you can substitute ground red pepper—but just one-eighth the amount, for it is far hotter and not as sweet.

Chicken Curry

4 servings

All of the flavors work together here; no spice is obvious, yet all are essential to the balance of this dish.

Remove the skin from:

3½ pounds chicken parts

Separate the legs into thighs and drumsticks; cut each breast half diagonally in half through the bone. Rinse the chicken and pat dry. Heat in a heavy, wide skillet over medium-high heat until shimmery:

2 tablespoons vegetable oil

Add and cook, stirring occasionally, until golden brown, 7 to 10 minutes:

1 large onion, thinly sliced

Add and cook, stirring, for 30 seconds:

2 teaspoons very finely minced garlic

2 teaspoons very finely minced peeled fresh ginger

1½ teaspoons *Garam Masala*, right

1 teaspoon ground turmeric

Add the chicken and cook, stirring, until the chicken loses its raw color,

2 to 3 minutes. Stir in:

½ cup low-fat yogurt

Cook, stirring occasionally, over high heat until the liquid has reduced and thickened and the oil separates and pools, 3 to 5 minutes. Stir in:

1 cup water

2 tablespoons chopped fresh cilantro

1 fresh serrano or jalapeño pepper, quartered lengthwise

¾ teaspoon salt

Reduce the heat so that the liquid bubbles gently, cover, and cook until the dark meat pieces release clear juices when pierced with a fork, 30 to 40 minutes. Remove the chicken to a platter or wide bowl and cover to keep warm. If the sauce is thin and runny, uncover the pot and boil over high heat to reduce and thicken it. Pour over the chicken. Serve with:

Hot cooked rice

Fresh Mint-Cilantro Chutney, right

Garam Masala

About 1 cup

Put in a heavy plastic bag and smash with a rolling pin until lightly crushed:

½ cup green or black cardamom pods

Break open the pods and pull out the tiny seeds. Discard the pods and combine the seeds with:

⅓ cup whole cloves

Scant ¼ cup cumin seeds

Scant ¼ cup black peppercorns

5 hefty (about ⅓-inch-thick) 3-inch-long cinnamon sticks

Grind the mixture to a powder in batches in a spice mill or electric coffee grinder. Store in an airtight container in a cool place.

Fresh Mint-Cilantro Chutney

About 1 cup

Combine in a food processor or blender and puree, stopping to scrape down the sides as needed:

1 cup lightly packed fresh mint leaves

½ cup lightly packed fresh cilantro leaves

½ cup coarsely chopped onions

3 small scallions, cut into small pieces

3 fresh jalapeño peppers, seeded and cut into small pieces

3 tablespoons water

1½ tablespoons fresh lemon juice

¼ teaspoon salt

Cover and refrigerate up to 1 day.

CARDAMOM

Cardamom is among the world's most ancient spices. The seedpods of true cardamom are oval and green, even after drying, and contain tiny seeds. In this natural state, the seeds are at the peak of quality—near black in color, with a strong, spicy fragrance and fresh, sweet taste. You can finely grind the seeds with a mortar and pestle as needed. The aroma of ground cardamom is elusive—a ghost of ginger, hints of coriander, white pepper, and perhaps nutmeg. In a pinch, bleached pods and their seeds can be substituted.

Doro Wat (Ethiopian Chicken in Red Pepper Sauce)

4 servings

The slow caramelizing of the onions requires patience and vigilance but is essential to the flavor of the dish.

Melt in a small, heavy saucepan over low heat:

8 tablespoons (1 stick) unsalted butter, cut into pieces

Add:

3 tablespoons coarsely chopped onions

1 tablespoon minced garlic

1 tablespoon minced peeled fresh ginger

One 1-inch piece cinnamon stick

¾ teaspoon ground turmeric

Heaping ¼ teaspoon whole cloves

⅛ teaspoon freshly grated or ground nutmeg

1 cardamom pod, crushed (optional)

Simmer, uncovered, until the sediment falls to the bottom of the pan and the onions are browned, 15 to 25 minutes. Strain through a fine-mesh sieve. Rinse:

3½ to 4½ pounds chicken parts

Remove and discard the skin. Separate the legs into thighs and drumsticks; cut each breast half diagonally in half through the bone. Rub the chicken pieces with:

½ lemon

Sprinkle generously with:

Salt

Cover loosely with wax paper and let stand at room temperature. Place a very large, heavy pan or Dutch oven over medium heat. Add to the dry pan:

3 to 4 cups finely chopped onions

Cook, stirring constantly, until the onions are very dry and beginning to brown, about 10 minutes. Reduce the heat and slowly pour in:

¼ cup water

Cook, stirring, until the onions are colored deep brown, about 10 minutes more. Be very careful not to let the onions burn. Remove the pan from the heat. In a separate bowl, make *berbere* by mixing together:

¼ cup paprika

1 to 3 teaspoons ground red pepper, or to taste

1 teaspoon ground ginger

½ teaspoon ground cinnamon

¼ teaspoon ground cloves or allspice

¼ teaspoon ground coriander (optional)

Stir into the onions, then add, making a smooth paste:

½ cup warm water

Stir in the spiced butter along with:

1 tablespoon minced garlic

1 tablespoon minced peeled fresh ginger

1½ teaspoons salt

1 teaspoon freshly grated or ground nutmeg

Bring to a simmer over medium heat and cook, stirring, for 1 minute. Add the chicken and turn to coat well. Return to a simmer, then reduce the heat so that the sauce barely bubbles. Cover and cook for 30 minutes, stirring often to prevent sticking. Stir in:

1½ cups dry wine or water

1 teaspoon ground black pepper

4 to 6 hard-boiled eggs, shelled (optional)

Cook, covered, until the chicken is very tender and the butter begins to rise to the top, about 10 minutes. Stir the butter back into the sauce. Serve with:

Hot cooked rice

Basic Cooked White Rice

3 cups; 4 servings

Use 2 cups water for soft, tender rice or 1¾ to 1⅞ cups for firmer grains. Use ¼ cup less, either way, when cooking medium-grain white rice. Do not stir, except as directed, as the rice will turn gummy.

I. Bring to a boil in a medium saucepan:

1¾ to 2 cups water

1 tablespoon butter or vegetable oil (optional)

¼ to ½ teaspoon salt

Add and stir once:

1 cup long-grain white rice

Cover and cook over very low heat until all the water is absorbed, 15 to 18 minutes. Do not lift the cover before the end of cooking. Let stand, covered, for 5 to 10 minutes before serving.

II. *This method is popular in the American South, Latin America, and parts of Europe.*

Spread in a large, broad, shallow, heavy saucepan to a depth of only 2 or 3 grains:

1 cup long-grain or medium-grain white rice

Add just enough liquid to cover the rice by ½ inch or the thickness of your hand. Bring to a gentle boil and stir once. Cook, uncovered, over low heat until the liquid is almost absorbed, about 5 minutes. Cover the saucepan and continue to cook for 15 to 18 minutes. Do not lift the cover before the end of cooking. Let stand, covered, for 5 to 10 minutes before serving.

Chicken Chili Verde

4 servings

Chili verde can be served with rice, beans, and corn tortillas or used as a filling for burritos, tacos, or enchiladas. You can make this recipe with 2 to 3 cups leftover chicken and 2 cups canned chicken broth.

Combine in a medium pan:

2½ pounds chicken thighs and/or drumsticks, or mixed chicken parts

4 cups Chicken Stock, 124, or 4 cups water and 1 teaspoon salt

Bring to a boil over high heat, then reduce the heat so that the liquid simmers gently. Cook, partially covered, for 30 minutes. Remove the chicken from the stock and let stand until cool enough to handle. Remove the skin and bones, keeping the meat in the largest chunks possible. Skim the fat from the stock with a spoon. (For an especially flavorful dish, chop the bones with a cleaver and return with the skin to the stock; simmer for 1 hour and degrease.)

Heat in a large, heavy pan over medium heat until shimmery:

2 tablespoons vegetable oil

Add:

1 cup chopped onions

¼ cup chopped celery

1 tablespoon chopped garlic

Cook, stirring occasionally, until the vegetables are tender, about 5 minutes. Sprinkle with:

2 teaspoons chili powder

1 teaspoon ground cumin

½ teaspoon dried oregano

½ teaspoon salt

Cook, stirring, until fragrant, about 1 minute. Remove the pan from the heat. Have ready:

1 cup canned tomatillos or 4 large or 6 medium fresh tomatillos

If using canned tomatillos, drain and chop. If using fresh, drop into about 6 cups of rapidly boiling water, boil for 1 minute, slip off the papery husks, and rinse well; cut out and discard the cores and dice the flesh. Add the tomatillos to the vegetable mixture. Separate the leaves and stems of:

1 large bunch cilantro

Finely chop the cilantro stems and leaves separately. Add the stems to the pan. Add 2 cups of the chicken stock along with:

3 fresh Anaheim or poblano peppers, roasted, opposite, peeled, and chopped, or one 7-ounce can diced green chilies, drained

2 fresh jalapeño peppers, seeded and finely chopped (optional)

Gently simmer the sauce, uncovered, for 10 minutes. Add the reserved chicken and ½ cup of the chopped cilantro leaves along with:

2 tablespoons fresh lime juice

Simmer for 5 to 15 minutes more, depending on how tender you prefer the chicken. Season with:

Salt to taste

Garnish with the remaining cilantro leaves.

New Mexican Chili Powder

About ½ cup

Combine and toast in a skillet over medium heat for 2 minutes:

5 tablespoons ground mild chili peppers, such as New Mexico, pasilla, or ancho

2 tablespoons dried oregano

1½ tablespoons ground cumin

½ teaspoon ground red pepper, or to taste

TOMATILLOS

Tomatillos look like small shiny green, yellow-green, or lavender tomatoes encased in parchment-paper husks. Tomatillos are picked underripe. They are related to gooseberries, and have a lemony tang. This tang lends sprightliness to sauces in Mexican cooking. Tomatillos are available at some supermarkets and Hispanic groceries. Select fruits that are firm and fill their husks, and avoid any that have come out of them. They can be stored, unwashed and unhusked, loose in the refrigerator crisper for weeks.

HOW TO ROAST PEPPERS

Roasting provides the best way to remove the skin of peppers. In addition, it softens their flesh, tempers the raw taste, and adds a delicious smokiness. Thick-walled peppers can be taken a step further and charred. Thinner-walled peppers—this includes most chilies— are better if blistered but not completely charred, or they will lose flesh when you peel them. Red peppers char faster than green ones, having more sugars in their flesh. Peppers that are a bit past their prime are perfect for roasting.

1 *Stove-Roasting:* Place whole peppers directly in the flames of your gas burner on its highest setting. Keep an eye on the peppers and turn them frequently with tongs, letting the peppers blister or char (do not pierce with a cooking fork, as juices will be lost). Continue until the entire surface is blistered.

2 *Broiler-Roasting:* Line a broiler pan with aluminum foil. Place whole peppers on the foil and brush with olive oil. Broil, turning as needed, until blackened on all sides.

3 Once they are blistered, lay peppers in a bowl and cover with a plate or plastic wrap. Their heat will create steam, which will loosen the skins. Try not to rinse peppers after roasting, for much of the smoky flavor is on the surface. Scrape off the skins with a knife. Make a slit down one side of the pepper, then run the tip of a small serrated knife around the stem underneath its base. Remove the core and seeds. Add any juices in the bottom of the bowl to the dish you are making.

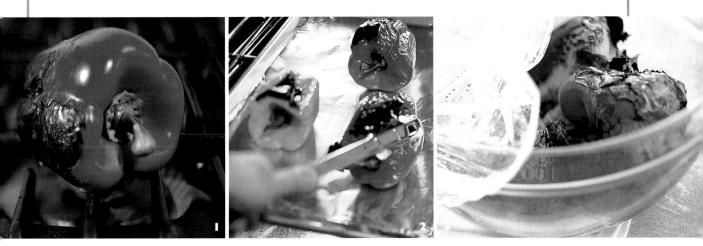

Chili Peppers

ANAHEIM

These long green chilies grow in the American Southwest and are likely the ones in a can labeled "green chilies." When fresh, they are light lime green to red. The flavor is reminiscent of bell peppers and green apples. They have a tough skin and a heat level that varies from mild to hot. Most measure 6 to 7 inches in length and 1½ inches wide at the stem end, tapering slightly before coming to a rather pointy tip.

JALAPEÑO

These stubby green to red chilies can vary in their heat from totally mild to hot varieties found in farmers' markets and their homeland of Veracruz, Mexico. This pepper has a bright green, juicy, grassy taste. Mature jalapeños, when smoked and dried, are known as chipotles. Fresh jalapeños measure about 2½ inches in length and ¾ inch wide at the stem end and taper a little before coming to a rather blunt tip.

POBLANO

This dark green pepper's flesh has a compact texture with a good (but varying) amount of heat. Use them roasted and peeled or whole as an edible vessel for a cheese filling, as in chiles rellenos. When dried, they usually are known as ancho chilies. Poblanos are used throughout Mexico. They measure 4 to 5 inches long and about 2½ inches wide at the stem end, tapering to a sharp point. They are also called pasilla.

Arroz con Pollo (Chicken and Rice)

4 servings

With a salad, arroz con pollo becomes a complete meal. Saffron threads color it a golden yellow.

Rinse and pat dry:

3½ to 4½ pounds chicken parts

Separate the chicken legs into thighs and drumsticks; cut each breast half diagonally in half through the bone. Season the chicken pieces with:

Salt and ground black pepper to taste

Heat in a wide, heavy pan large enough to hold the chicken pieces in a single layer over medium-high heat until shimmery:

2 tablespoons vegetable or olive oil

Add the chicken pieces and brown well on all sides, 7 to 10 minutes. Remove the chicken from the pan. Pour off all but 3 tablespoons of the fat. Reduce the heat to medium-low and add:

2 cups chopped onions
1 green bell pepper, diced (optional)
4 ounces smoked ham, finely diced (about ½ cup)

Cook, stirring occasionally, until the onions are tender but not brown, about 5 minutes. Add:

2 cups medium- or long-grain white rice

Cook, stirring, until the grains are coated with fat. Add:

1 tablespoon minced garlic
1 tablespoon paprika
1 teaspoon salt
½ teaspoon ground black pepper

Cook, stirring, for 1 minute. Add:

3 cups *Chicken Stock*, 124
½ teaspoon dried oregano (optional)

¼ teaspoon loosely packed saffron threads (optional)

Bring to a boil over high heat, scraping the bottom of the pan with a wooden spoon to loosen the browned bits. Nestle the chicken pieces in the rice and pour in any accumulated juices. Cover the pan tightly and simmer over medium-low heat for 20 minutes. Stir in:

1 cup cooked fresh peas or unthawed frozen peas
⅓ cup drained bottled pimientos or roasted red peppers, cut into thin 1-inch-long strips
¼ cup chopped pitted brine-cured green olives

Cover and cook until the rice is tender, about 10 minutes more. Taste and adjust the seasonings.

SAFFRON THREADS

The golden red stigmas of the autumn crocus contribute extraordinary fragrance, aromatic flavor, and golden color. The tiny threads are strong. Just the right amount, and the dish is perfumed. Two or three stigmas too many, and the dish is bitter. When selecting saffron, the deeper the color, the finer the quality. The way to glean the most from the threads and to spread their color evenly is to make an infusion with liquid that can be used in the dish. Add the saffron called for to as much hot (not boiling) liquid as you can use—the more liquid, the farther the flavor will be carried. Let stand until the color is deep and bright and the aroma fills the kitchen.

Chicken Tagine with Chickpeas

4 servings

Tagine refers to the cooking vessel in which Moroccan cooks prepare this and other similar stews. A hint of cinnamon provides a characteristically North African flavor. This dish is quickly and easily prepared in a single pot with ingredients that you are likely to have on hand.

Remove the skin from, rinse, and pat dry:

3½ to 4 pounds chicken parts

Heat in a large, heavy pan over medium-high heat until fragrant and golden:

2 tablespoons unsalted butter

Lightly brown the chicken in 2 batches in the hot butter and remove to a plate. Add to the pan:

2 cups chopped onions
½ cup chopped scallions

Cook, stirring often, until the onions are tender, 5 to 7 minutes. Stir in:

One 19-ounce can chickpeas, drained and lightly rinsed
1 cup water
1 tablespoon minced garlic
1 teaspoon ground ginger
¾ teaspoon salt
½ teaspoon ground black pepper
½ teaspoon ground cinnamon
⅛ to ¼ teaspoon ground red pepper

Return the chicken pieces with all accumulated juices to the pan and gently turn to coat.

Bring the mixture to a boil, then reduce the heat so that the liquid just simmers. Cover tightly and cook, turning the chicken once or twice, until the dark meat releases clear juices when pierced with a fork, 35 to 45 minutes. Remove from the heat and stir in:

½ cup chopped fresh parsley and/or cilantro

Season with:

Salt and ground black pepper to taste

ABOUT **FRIED** CHICKEN

*B*ecause fat contains no moisture, pan-frying, oven-frying, and deep-frying are all technically dry-heat cooking methods. But our intuition tells us that these techniques are fundamentally different. Simply put, oil protects food from drying out, especially in deep-frying, where submerging food in oil traps in moisture, steaming the food inside while browning the surface.

You can produce excellent fried chicken in a variety of ways, including frying it in the oven. Fried chicken is defined as much by the cooking process as by the result, which should be juicy, succulent chicken covered in a crispy crust that is not at all greasy.

Crispy-Crunchy Deep-Fried Chicken, 90

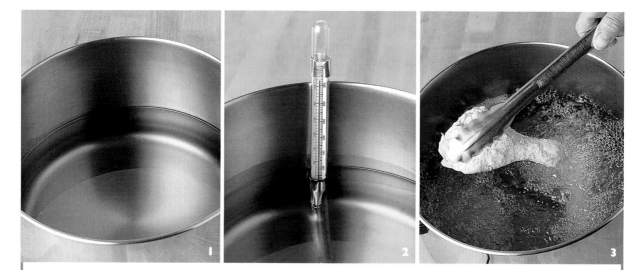

RULES FOR DEEP-FRYING

• Done with care, chicken can emerge from hot oil crisp on the outside, moist within. Although intensely hot, the process is brief, so the food must already be tender to cook properly. To add a crunchy coating and to protect its tender flesh, chicken is usually battered before cooking.

• Any deep kettle or saucepan, preferably a heavy one, serves nicely for deep-frying. The kettle should have a flat bottom, so that it sits securely on the heating unit. A short pot handle is desirable, to avoid the danger of accidentally overturning the hot oil. In case the fat should catch fire, have a metal lid handy to drop over the kettle. You may also smother the flame with salt or baking soda, but never use water, as this will only spread the fire.

• Always use fresh oil each time you fry.

• It is not wise to skimp on the amount of fat. There must always be enough to cover the food and to permit it to move freely in the kettle. There must also be room for the quick bubbling up that occurs naturally when frying items with high moisture content. Never fill any container more than half full with fat (1).

• Remember also to heat the fat gradually (always uncovered) so that any unexpected moisture in it will have slowly evaporated by the time it reaches the required temperature.

• Nothing is more important in frying than proper temperatures. For judging the temperature of the fat, use a deep-fry thermometer, no other (2). Temperatures will vary slightly depending on the recipe and the food you are frying. Above all, do not wait for the oil to smoke before adding the food. This is hard on the oil, since smoke indicates that it is breaking down, and the crust that forms on the food is likely to be overbrowned on the surface before the inside is cooked through. Food introduced into fat that is not hot enough to crust immediately, however, will tend to be grease-soaked.

• Whenever possible, food should be at room temperature and as dry as possible when introduced into the kettle. Unbattered raw pieces, especially moist ones, should be patted between paper towels before cooking. It is generally best to immerse food gently (3). For good results, pieces of food to be fried should be uniform in size; small pieces, obviously, will cook through faster than large ones. Fry in several small batches rather than in one large one. The cooked food may be kept hot on a rack set over a pan or on a paper-lined pan in an oven set at very low heat.

• After frying one batch of food, always let the oil temperature come up again to the required heat.

• Skim out bits of food or crumbs frequently as they collect in the fat during frying. If allowed to remain, they induce foaming, discolor the fat, and affect the flavor of the food. Have paper towels ready on which to drain the cooked food and so rid it of excess fat before serving.

Fried Chicken

4 servings

This chicken has the crackling crisp skin and distinctive mahogany color that are the hallmarks of this dish as prepared by the best Southern cooks. Use a cast-iron skillet if possible, for it allows the chicken to achieve the prized deep color without charring. Frying the chicken in vegetable shortening rather than oil gives the crust a snapping crispness and, because shortening is more highly refined than oil, the odor-causing compounds are removed and it leaves less odor in the kitchen. The crust will stay crisper longer if you drain the chicken on a rack rather than on a paper bag or paper towels.

Rinse and pat dry:

3½ to 4 pounds chicken parts

Separate the chicken legs into thighs and drumsticks; cut each breast half diagonally in half through the bone. Stir together in a large bowl:

1½ cups buttermilk

1 teaspoon salt

½ teaspoon ground black pepper

Add the chicken and turn to coat well. Cover the bowl with plastic wrap or remove the chicken and buttermilk to a sealable plastic bag. Refrigerate for 2 to 12 hours. Shake to mix in a doubled brown paper bag:

2 cups all-purpose flour

2 teaspoons salt

1 teaspoon ground black pepper

Pinch of ground red pepper (optional)

Shake the chicken a few pieces at a time in the bag until well coated. Let dry on a rack at room temperature for 15 to 30 minutes. Place a deep, heavy skillet, preferably cast iron, large enough to hold the chicken pieces in a single layer over medium-high heat and add:

3 cups solid vegetable shortening

There should be enough shortening in the skillet to measure about ½ inch. Heat until a small corner of a chicken piece causes vigorous bubbling when dipped into the fat, about 350°F on a deep-fry thermometer. Being careful not to spatter yourself, gently lay the chicken pieces skin side down in the hot fat and cover. Cook for 10 minutes, checking after 5 minutes and moving the pieces if they are coloring unevenly or turning the heat down if the chicken is browning too quickly. (At this point, the fat should be bubbling and register between 250° and 300°F on a thermometer.) Turn the chicken pieces with tongs and cook, uncovered, until the second side is richly browned, 10 to 12 minutes more. Remove the chicken to a rack set over a baking sheet. If not serving immediately, remove the chicken, still on the rack, to an oven warmed at the lowest setting. If you wish, prepare in the pan:

Poultry Pan Sauce or Gravy, 27

Chicken that is not to be served hot may be safely held at room temperature, still on the rack and loosely covered with wax paper, for several hours. It will be crisper and juicier than if chilled. Leftovers, of course, must be refrigerated.

BUTTERMILK

Sour milks and creams, a group to which buttermilk can be added, have long played an important part in cooking. Because they contain lactic acid, they are often used to tenderize foods in cooking. Buttermilk, once the residue left over from making butter, is today made by adding a bacterial culture to skim milk. Thus the word "buttermilk" today means cultured buttermilk. A buttermilk marinade is traditionally used to promote tenderness in fried chicken.

Crispy-Crunchy Deep-Fried Chicken

4 servings

If plain fried chicken is not crusty enough to suit your taste, try this instead. This chicken is almost as much crust as it is meat. For this recipe, you might consider buying a small chicken and cutting it into ten serving pieces yourself (see How to Cut Up a Chicken, 12). *Packs of mixed parts often contain oversized pieces, which can become excessively dark on the outside before the chicken has cooked through.*

Rinse and pat dry:

3½ pounds chicken parts, or
  1 whole chicken (about
  3½ pounds), cut into
  10 serving pieces

Separate the legs into thighs and drumsticks; cut each breast half diagonally in half through the bone. Sprinkle the chicken very generously with:

Salt and ground black pepper
  to taste

Whisk thoroughly in a medium bowl:

2 large eggs
⅓ cup plus 1 tablespoon milk
1 teaspoon salt

Mix together on a plate:

1½ cups all-purpose flour
2 teaspoons salt
2 teaspoons ground black pepper

Heat in a deep-fat fryer or deep, heavy pot to 350°F:

3 pounds solid vegetable
  shortening

There should be at least 2 inches fat in the pot. Toss the breast pieces and wings in the flour mixture, then remove to the egg mixture and turn until thoroughly moistened on all sides. One at a time, lift the pieces out of the egg, letting the excess drip off, roll in the flour mixture until completely coated, and slip into the hot fat. Fry for 10 minutes, turning the pieces several times with tongs and keeping the fat between 320° and 360°F. Remove the pieces to a baking sheet lined with paper towels, quickly turn to blot up the excess oil, then slip into a barely warm oven. Repeat the same procedure with the thighs and drumsticks, frying the pieces for 15 minutes rather than 10. The liver may be coated and fried just until golden, about 2 minutes. Serve immediately.

Velouté Sauce

About 2 cups

A velouté, named for its velvety texture, is made exclusively with any "white" or light-colored stock. The resulting sauce is more ivory-colored than béchamel, which is made with milk. Because it is made with stock, a velouté is slightly translucent. Traditionally, it is served with the same kind of food that was used to make it—for example, made with chicken stock and served with chicken. A velouté can also be used to bind ingredients. Allowing the sauce to simmer gently for an extra 15 minutes will remove any trace of a floury taste.

Heat, stirring occasionally, in a small saucepan over medium heat until hot:

2½ cups *Chicken Stock, 124*

Meanwhile, melt in a medium, heavy saucepan over low heat:

3 tablespoons butter, preferably unsalted

Stir in:

3 tablespoons all-purpose flour

Cook over low heat, stirring constantly with a wooden spoon or spatula, until the roux is fragrant and ivory colored or just lightly darkened, about 6 minutes. Remove from the heat and let cool for 1 minute. Gradually whisk in the stock along with:

¼ cup minced mushrooms (optional)

Return the saucepan to the heat and bring the sauce slowly to a simmer, whisking to prevent lumps. Cook the sauce, stirring often and skimming any skin that forms on the surface, over medium-low heat, without boiling, until it is thick enough to coat the back of a spoon, about 20 minutes. Strain through a fine-mesh sieve, if desired. Season with:

Salt and ground black pepper
  to taste

Just before serving, whisk in:

1 to 2 tablespoons unsalted
  butter, softened

Chicken Croquettes

4 servings

A classic croquette is a mixture of very thick velouté sauce and cooked poultry that is shaped, breaded, and deep-fried. This old-fashioned but extremely satisfying dish may be served with a sauce or a squeeze of lemon juice. Accompany the croquettes with a green vegetable and mashed potatoes or rice.

Prepare using 4 tablespoons unsalted butter and ¼ cup flour:

½ recipe *Velouté Sauce*, opposite

Melt in a medium saucepan over medium-low heat:

1 tablespoon unsalted butter

Stir in:

1 cup chopped onions

Cook, stirring often, until tender but still crunchy, 7 to 10 minutes. Add the reserved sauce and cook for 1 minute. Scrape the sauce into a large bowl and combine thoroughly with:

2½ cups chopped skinless, cooked chicken

¼ cup chopped fresh parsley

½ teaspoon ground white or black pepper

½ teaspoon dried thyme

⅛ teaspoon ground nutmeg

Salt to taste

Press a sheet of plastic wrap directly on the surface of the mixture and refrigerate until very cold and firm, at least 2 hours. Spread in an even layer on 2 separate plates:

1½ cups fresh breadcrumbs

½ cup all-purpose flour

Whisk together in a wide shallow bowl:

2 large eggs

Drop a generous ¼-cup scoop of the croquette mixture onto the flour and gently roll until the rough ball is evenly coated. Roll in the beaten egg, then transfer to the breadcrumbs and roll until coated on all sides. While rolling, shape the croquette into an oval, cylinder, or pyramid. Set aside on a plate. Repeat with the remaining mixture to make 8 croquettes.

Heat to 375°F in a deep-fryer or deep, heavy pot over medium-high heat:

8 cups vegetable oil or 3 pounds solid vegetable shortening

Gently drop 4 croquettes in the hot fat and fry until deep brown on all sides, 3 to 4 minutes. Remove with a slotted spoon and drain on paper towels. Fry the remaining croquettes in the same manner. Arrange on 4 plates or on a platter and serve with:

Lemon wedges or cranberry sauce

Oven-Fried Chicken with a Cornmeal Crust

4 servings

Oven-frying delivers a crisp, crunchy crust with a minimum of fat. This chicken is terrific served at room temperature as part of a summer picnic or as leftovers for lunch. If serving it cold, you can remove the skin before coating and baking, which also reduces the fat substantially. The marinated chicken baked without the coating is also delicious and quick to prepare. Lemon zest and chili powder add a nice kick.

Rinse and pat dry:

3½ pounds chicken parts

Whisk together in a bowl large enough to hold the chicken:

¾ cup buttermilk or whole-milk or low-fat yogurt

¼ cup strained fresh lemon juice

¼ cup olive oil

2 tablespoons finely minced shallots

1 tablespoon finely minced fresh thyme or rosemary, or
 1 teaspoon dried

2 teaspoons salt

2 teaspoons chili powder

1 teaspoon grated lemon zest (optional)

Add the chicken to the yogurt mixture and turn to coat. Cover and refrigerate for 2 to 4 hours.

Position a rack in the upper third of the oven. Preheat the oven to 425°F. Lightly oil a baking sheet.

Combine in a wide, shallow bowl:

⅔ cup grated Parmesan or aged Monterey Jack cheese

½ cup dry unseasoned breadcrumbs

½ cup cornmeal

3 tablespoons minced fresh parsley

1 teaspoon chili powder

1 teaspoon salt

½ teaspoon ground black pepper

Remove the chicken from the marinade and shake off the excess. Whisk together in a shallow bowl:

2 large eggs

2 tablespoons melted butter

Dip the chicken pieces in the egg mixture, then coat with the cornmeal mixture, patting with your fingers to make the crumbs adhere. The chicken can be prepared to this point up to 3 hours in advance and kept, uncovered, in the refrigerator. Arrange the chicken skin side up on the baking sheet. If you wish, drizzle over the chicken:

2 to 3 tablespoons melted butter or olive oil

Bake until the chicken is crisp and golden, 35 to 40 minutes. Serve immediately or at room temperature.

CORNMEAL

Corn on the cob, the only grain eaten fresh from the field, previews the subtle sweetness of cornmeal. Cornmeal is ground from dried corn in one of two ways. Simply ground and available in coarse, medium, or fine grind, it can be used in any recipe unless otherwise specified. Stoneground cornmeal retains the oily germ and the starchy endosperm, has a much higher fiber and mineral content, and is usually called for by name. It must be refrigerated. The more commonly available enriched degerminated cornmeal has lost its germ and thus has a more stable shelf life.

Gorgonzola-Stuffed Chicken Breasts

4 servings

If you have the time, refrigerate the coated chicken breasts, covered, for up to 4 hours. This will help the crust adhere while the chicken is cooking (opposite).

In a medium, heavy skillet, heat:

3 tablespoons olive oil

Add:

3 medium onions, sliced

Reduce the heat to low and cook until deep brown, about 25 minutes. Transfer the onions to a bowl and let cool. Stir in:

½ cup crumbled Gorgonzola cheese

⅓ cup chopped walnuts, toasted

Cover and refrigerate until ready to use.

Lay smooth side down on a work surface and flatten to a ¼-inch thickness:

4 boneless, skinless chicken breast halves (about 1½ pounds)

Spoon one-quarter of the filling onto each breast and spread to within ½ inch of the edges. Fold about ½ inch of each long side over the filling. Press down firmly. Roll the breasts starting with the narrow end and keeping the folded edges tucked in. Secure with a toothpick. Combine in a wide, shallow dish:

½ cup finely chopped walnuts

½ cup cornmeal

Salt and ground black pepper to taste

Roll the chicken breasts in:

3 tablespoons butter, melted

Then roll in the cornmeal mixture to cover, pressing the coating with your hands. In a medium skillet, over medium heat, heat until foaming:

2 tablespoons butter

1 tablespoon olive oil

Add the breasts, seam side down. Cook, turning them every few minutes, until the crust is well browned and the chicken feels firm when pressed, about 18 minutes.

TOASTING NUTS

Toasting nuts crisps them and brings out their flavor. To toast nuts in the oven: Spread them blanched or unblanched on an ungreased baking sheet and bake in a 325° oven for 5 to 7 minutes, depending on the size of the nuts, checking and stirring often to prevent burning. To toast nuts on top of the stove: Place them in a dry skillet over medium heat and cook, stirring or shaking the pan frequently to prevent burning, until they just begin to release their fragrance, about 4 minutes.

To avoid loss of flavor and toughening, do not overtoast, as nuts tend to darken further and become crisper as they cool. Let toasted nuts cool completely before processing them in a food processor or blender. Toasted nuts can be stored in a cool, dry place for up to 2 weeks.

Pan-Fried Chicken

4 servings

The quickest and simplest of all fried chicken recipes. Because it is not coated with flour, the chicken does not have a true crust, but the skin is deliciously brown and crispy.

Rinse and pat dry:

3½ to 4 pounds chicken parts

Season generously with:

Salt and ground black pepper to taste

Heat in a large, heavy skillet over medium-high heat until golden and fragrant:

1 tablespoon unsalted butter

1 tablespoon vegetable oil

Arrange the chicken pieces skin side down in a single layer in the skillet. Fry until the chicken is nicely browned on the bottom and detaches itself easily from the skillet, about 5 minutes. Turn the chicken with tongs and cook until nicely browned on the second side, about 5 minutes more. Reduce the heat to medium and continue to cook the chicken, turning often, until the dark meat pieces exude clear juices when pricked with a fork, about 20 minutes more. Remove the chicken to a platter. If you wish, prepare in the pan:

Poultry Pan Sauce or Gravy, 27

ABOUT **GRILLED** CHICKEN

*T*he grilling techniques that yield perfect burgers and steaks do not always work for chicken. Burgers and steaks really need nothing more than a red-hot fire, but grilled chicken—with its bones and skin and combination of light or dark meat—requires a more complicated management of heat.

The same hot fire that gives a steak its pleasing brown crust will char bone-in chicken pieces before cooking them through, and chicken fat dripping onto the hot coals will quickly spark a conflagration. No wonder so many of today's cooks opt for boneless, skinless chicken breasts—no pesky bones, no fatty skin, no irregular shapes to contend with—but the perks have their price. Both bones and skin add flavor to the meat, and the skin also protects the meat from the harsh heat and, when cooked to the proper crispness, adds richness and welcome textural contrast.

Grill-Smoked Jamaican Jerk Chicken, 108

Grilling Chicken

Chicken is cooked on an outdoor grill in one of two ways: either directly over the hot coals (grilling) or *opposite* the coals, which are arranged on the grill bottom across from the chicken (grill-roasting or barbecuing). Grilling requires a rather cool fire and an unheated spot on the grill to which the chicken may quickly be pulled in the case of flare-ups. It also demands the cook's undivided attention.

Grill-roasting is easier but does not crisp and brown the chicken skin, and it imparts a milder flavor and softer, more barbecuelike texture than grilling. For those who want the flavor of grilling and the ease of grill-roasting, a combination of both techniques can be used, much like oven-searing at a high temperature, then roasting at a lower temperature to ensure even cooking. The chicken is cooked over moderately hot coals until its skin begins to crisp and render fat; then it is removed to a spot opposite the fire, covered, and allowed to cook through by indirect heat.

Butterflied whole chickens and skin-on chicken parts can be grilled, grill-roasted, or cooked by a combination of techniques. Because of their short cooking time, boneless, skinless chicken parts should be grilled. (They also benefit from a marinade, which offers the flavor and protection normally provided by the skin.) Whole chickens, however, must be grill-roasted, or else they will burn before cooking through.

The recipes in this section can be adapted for use with a gas grill. Turn both burners on high to preheat the grill rack, then turn off one of the burners. If grilling, place the chicken on the heated side, reserving the opposite side as a safety area. If grill-roasting, place the chicken on the unheated side of the rack and cover the grill; the turned-on burner will provide the heat. If the grill is equipped with an upper rack set above the grill rack, you can turn both burners on and grill-roast on the upper rack or use this rack as a safety area when grilling.

Grilling Equipment

Most outdoor grills fall into one of two categories: open or covered. Open grills range in size and portability from the simple, small hibachi to large built-in units. An open grill is most useful if it has a heavy grate (to transfer heat and give beautiful grill marks) and an adjustable firebox or grate (to help control the intensity of heat). Covered grills come in many styles, but the covered kettle grill ranks high. Neither the charcoal grate on which the coals rest nor the cooking grate is adjustable, and the most popular units were designed to be used with the lid, to reduce the possibility of flare-ups and to speed cooking by circulating heat around the food.

Gas grills have come a long way in the last few years, most notably in burning fuel more efficiently and in their ability to achieve the higher temperatures crucial for a delectable brown crust. Generally speaking, gas grills take about 10 minutes to preheat.

Unfortunately the so-called "stovetop grills"—basically some variety of metal grid that fits over a stove burner, equipped with a pan to catch dripping grease—do not get hot enough to really grill. If you want to grill inside and you have a fireplace, consider the Tuscan grill. Although difficult to find, this handy device consists of a simple metal frame that holds an adjustable grilling grate, suitable for use in indoor fireplaces. To rig one of your own, remove the grill surface from any standard outdoor grill and support it in the fireplace above the coals with bricks.

SPIT ROASTING

Spit and rotisserie cooking (the terms are interchangeable) are perfect for small or large fowl. Some grills include a spit, which is usually protected from wind by a metal shield on three sides. Consult the directions that come with a spit to determine the maximum weight it will support—probably up to fifteen pounds for fowl. Smaller birds should be strung traversely on the spit, larger ones head to tail along the spit's axis. Remember that because of the high heat of spit roasting, the weight losses due to shrinkage can be great and flare-ups from dripping fat frequent. Flare-ups can be avoided in part by careful trimming of surplus fat. Some short flare-ups may be desired for browning.

Starting the Fire

Starter fluid or presoaked charcoal briquettes should be avoided. Because fumes are released throughout the cooking process, the taste of the food can be affected.

To start a fire in the simplest fashion, crumple several sheets of newspaper in the bottom of the grill beneath the fire grate, set the grate back in place over the newspapers, and lay several handfuls of twigs or kindling on the grate. Next top the twigs with a rather loose tepee-shaped arrangement of slightly larger twigs (or several handfulls of charcoal, if that is your fuel of choice) and light the newspaper. When the wood or charcoal is well lit, add additional fuel.

If the fuel is charcoal, you can start your fire with an electrical coil starter instead of paper and twigs. These electrical coils, attached to a power cord by means of a plastic handle, are reliable and consistent.

The chimney starter is the paragon of efficiency. It is a sheet metal cylinder, open at both ends, with a grid set inside the flue. Fill the bottom section with crumpled newspaper, then fill the top with charcoal and light the newspaper. When the charcoal is red hot, dump it out and put as much additional charcoal as you want on top of it.

Whatever lighting method you use, light the fire in advance to ensure an even, flameless fire of the proper temperature. Allow time for the fuel to get fiery red and then die down until it is just covered with gray ash.

FUEL FOR THE FIRE

Grilling has become synonymous with little pillow-shaped charcoal briquettes, available in every supermarket. Because they are not pure charcoal but rather a combination of charcoal, sawdust, powdered scrap lumber, starch, and additives, briquettes can impart unpleasant flavors. Hardwood lump charcoal, made by burning hardwood in a closed container with very little oxygen, is worth searching out in hardware and specialty stores. These chunks of almost pure carbon light more easily, give heat that is more responsive to changes in oxygen, and burn cleaner and hotter than briquettes. A wide variety of wood chips on the market, ranging from mesquite to cherry to hickory, can be added to glowing charcoal to give a smokier, wood-fire flavor. But unless the food spends more than a few minutes on the grill, the smoke from the chips will have little time to penetrate it.

Grill Precautions

For safety's sake always set your grill on level ground in the largest possible open space, away from walls, wooden fences, or tree branches, or anything else that might easily catch fire. Keep toddlers well away from the grill, and do not let older children run or play too close to the grilling area. If using any charcoal-fired equipment, do so with adequate ventilation, where the carbon monoxide fumes can be carried off completely; do not ever use charcoal grills in a house, tent, cabin, garage, or other enclosed area. Insufficient ventilation may prove fatal. Never light the fire with gasoline, and never spray lighter fluid onto lit coals. It is always a good idea to have handy a fire extinguisher or a bucket of sand. Remember, fire goes out without oxygen, so fires in covered grills can be extinguished by closing the lid and vents.

Grill-Roasting Whole Birds

In this hybrid method, whole birds and the like are roasted by the indirect heat of the fire in a covered grill, as if in a smoky oven. To grill-roast, build a fire in your grill in the usual manner and push all the coals to the sides. On the other side, place a drip pan if you wish to collect juices or fill the cooking kettle with the steam from aromatic liquids. When you put the food on the cooking grate, place it over the side that has no coals and over the drip pan if you are using one. Then set the grill cover in place, making sure no portion of the item you are cooking is directly over the fire. Adjust the vents as necessary to maintain the temperature between 250° and 300°F; an oven thermometer, set close to the food, will help you determine the temperature of the environment.

Grill-Roasted Whole Chicken

4 servings

Grill-roasting produces a chicken with perfectly cooked breast meat and a delicious smoked taste. No seasoning other than salt is really required, but if you wish, you can rub the chicken with herbs and garlic (see Roasted Chicken with Herbs and Garlic, 28). Alternatively, you can brush the chicken with barbecue sauce after it has roasted for 45 minutes.

Remove the neck and giblets from, then rinse and pat dry:

1 whole chicken (3½ to
  4½ pounds)

Generously rub the neck and body cavities and sprinkle the skin with:

Salt

Perform a simple truss, 18, or tie the legs together. Brush the chicken all over with:

2 tablespoons olive oil or melted
  butter

Open the vents on the bottom of the grill completely. Ignite 55 to 65 charcoal briquettes and heat until covered with white ash. Divide the coals in half and push half to each side of the grill. Replace the grill rack and arrange the chicken breast side up directly on the rack midway between the two piles of coals. Cover the grill and open the cover vents completely. After 45 minutes, if you like, you can brush the chicken with:

½ to 1 cup Barbecue Sauce, 120

Roast until the thigh exudes clear juices when pricked deeply with a fork and registers 175° to 180°F on an instant-read thermometer, 60 to 80 minutes. Let the chicken stand for 10 to 15 minutes before carving.

OLIVE OIL

Olive oil replaces what used to be called "pure olive oil." The best grades of olive oil are made simply: The fruit is crushed and the oil collected. Buy the freshest olive oil possible. Pressing is done from midautumn to January, depending upon origin. Usually these oils reach the market by early spring. Store in a cool, dark place and use within one year. Keep oil away from heat and light.

Chicken Kebabs

8 kebabs; 4 to 6 servings

Composed of chunks of marinated chicken and an array of multicolored vegetables, kebabs are best grilled over direct heat. Since vegetables, generally speaking, cook rather slowly, cut them in pieces no bigger than the chicken chunks.

Prepare:

¾ cup Fresh Herb Vinaigrette, right

Or stir together in a medium bowl:

½ cup olive oil

3 tablespoons strained fresh lemon juice

2 to 3 cloves garlic, minced

1 teaspoon salt

1 teaspoon ground black pepper

Pour half of the marinade into another medium bowl. Rinse and pat dry, then dip into the marinade and turn to coat well:

4 boneless, skinless chicken breast halves or 6 boneless, skinless chicken thighs, cut into 1-inch cubes

Cover and refrigerate for at least 30 minutes or up to 2 hours. When you are ready to grill the kebabs, add to the remaining marinade and turn to coat:

1 large red onion, cut into ½-inch chunks

16 small mushrooms

16 cherry tomatoes

1 red, yellow, or green bell pepper, cut into 1-inch pieces, or
2 small zucchini or summer squash, halved lengthwise and sliced ½ inch thick

Thread the meat and vegetables onto 8 skewers, leaving a little space between the pieces to allow for even cooking.

Heat about 50 charcoal briquettes until covered with white ash. Spread the coals on one side of the grill to make a medium-hot fire. Replace the grill rack and cover the grill until the rack is hot, about 5 minutes. Arrange the skewers on the hot rack opposite the coals and place a strip of aluminum foil under the exposed ends of the skewers. Grill for 4 minutes, then turn and grill until the vegetables are crisp-tender and browned along the edges and the chicken is opaque in the center, 3 to 4 minutes more.

Fresh Herb Vinaigrette

About 1½ cups

If garlic flavor is desired, mash together until a paste is formed:

1 small clove garlic, peeled
2 to 3 pinches of salt

Remove to a small bowl or a jar with a tight-fitting lid. Add and whisk or shake until will blended:

⅓ to ½ cup red wine vinegar or fresh lemon juice
⅓ cup minced or finely snipped fresh herbs (basil, dill, parsley, chives, and/or thyme)
1 shallot, minced
1 teaspoon Dijon mustard (optional)
Salt and ground black pepper to taste

Add in a slow, steady stream, whisking constantly, or add to the jar and shake until smooth:

1 cup extra-virgin olive oil

Taste and adjust the seasonings. Use at once or cover and refrigerate.

THREADING KEBABS

Remember to soak wooden or bamboo skewers in water for at least 30 minutes before use to prevent them from charring. If you thread big pieces of poultry and vegetables onto two parallel skewers in the making of each kebab, the pieces will stay put when the kebabs are turned, ensuring even cooking. Although less eye-pleasing, segregating chicken and vegetables on separate skewers guarantees that both will be cooked just right. Whatever you do, be sure to thread the chicken and vegetables on the skewers loosely, for neither will cook evenly in cramped quarters. Firm vegetables such as carrots, potatoes, cauliflower, and broccoli should be steamed until nearly tender before threading on a kebab. Keeping this in mind, almost all vegetables will work threaded on kebabs.

Cooking in Ashes

Ash cooking is best done in a fireplace or campfire. The food you are preparing should be cut into relatively small pieces so that it will cook through before browning too much at the edges. And it is a good idea to keep the batches of food small, so the packets are not too unwieldy to take in and out of the coals.

Whether wood or charcoal is the fuel, the fire should have passed its peak of intensity and be dying down—nothing but glowing coals covered with gray ash. Sweep the coals to the side, leaving your "cooking surface" covered with hot ashes. Lay in the packets and surround with the coals. The only way to check for doneness is to open a packet and take a peek.

WRAPPING CHICKEN FOR ASH COOKING

Bone-in chicken is a wonderful candidate for ash cooking. Wrapping chicken properly requires three sheets of heavy-duty aluminum foil, each about 2 feet long.

Start by spreading the food over the center of the first sheet, then lay the second length on top. Fold the edges of the two sheets together on all sides, closing the pack, then roll them up until they bump into the food, forming a ridge around its perimeter (**1**).

Place the pack folded side up in the center of the third sheet of foil and fold the four sides over the top of the packet, one after the other (**2**).

Ash-Roasted Chicken Thighs

3 to 6 servings

In this recipe, chicken thighs are triple-wrapped in foil and cooked directly on hot coals rather than on a grill rack. On a wintry night, when outdoor grilling is a distant pleasant memory, you might try cooking the chicken in your fireplace, burying the chicken in the embers surrounding the fire, not directly under it. The same technique can be employed with a campfire. This recipe can be multiplied to serve as many people as you wish, but wrap only two thighs per packet to guarantee easy handling.

Rinse, pat dry, and remove the skin from:

6 bone-in chicken thighs

Sprinkle generously with:
Salt and ground black pepper to taste
Have ready:
¼ cup minced fresh parsley
6 cloves garlic, thinly sliced
1 lemon, very thinly sliced
Cut a sheet of wide, heavy-duty foil about 18 inches long. Place 2 thighs in the center of the sheet, sprinkle with parsley and garlic, and top with 2 or 3 lemon slices. Cover with a second sheet of foil, also 18 inches long. Crimp the edges of the two sheets to seal securely, then roll the edges in toward the center to make an 8- to 9-inch square packet. Wrap

the packet in a third sheet of foil to seal completely. Repeat with the remaining thighs, making 3 packets altogether.
Heat 55 to 65 charcoal briquettes until covered with white ash. Push the coals to one side of the grill, arrange the chicken packets in a single layer over the bottom of the grill, and scatter the coals in an even layer over the top of the packets. Cook for 35 minutes. Remove the packets from the coals with tongs and let stand for 10 minutes. Open the foil carefully to avoid being burned by the steam.

Spicy Chicken Hobo Pack with Lime and Chili Peppers

4 servings

Roasting food in the embers of a dying fire is one of the easiest and oldest ways of cooking in the world—and it is still a favorite technique in Boy Scout and Girl Scout camps throughout the United States, where foil-wrapped meals are known as "hobo packs." There is an element of unpredictability in cooking these packets (which can contain just about any combination of meat and vegetables), but that's part of the fun, and there is no denying the intrinsic appeal of this method to the primitive cook in all of us.

Combine in a large bowl and toss well:

4 bone-in chicken breast halves, skin removed

8 small new potatoes

12 garlic cloves, unpeeled

1 lime, sliced into very thin rounds

⅓ cup chopped fresh cilantro or parsley

1 teaspoon minced fresh chili peppers

¼ cup olive oil

Salt and ground black pepper to taste

Place in the center of a sheet of heavy-duty aluminum foil about 2 feet long. Cover with a second sheet of foil and roll the edges together on all sides to seal. Place in the center of a third length of foil and fold it up around the pack. Prepare a medium-hot charcoal fire. Place the pack on the bottom of the grill or fireplace, and pile coals up on all sides. Cook for 30 to 35 minutes, depending on the intensity of the coals. Remove from the coals, carefully unroll the foil, and serve at once.

Grilled Spice-Rubbed Chicken with Lemon and Garlic Oil

4 servings

This recipe (opposite) calls for bone-in breasts, but mixed chicken parts or boneless, skinless breasts or thighs can be substituted. Since boneless, skinless parts cook more quickly, grill them directly over the coals until completely done, 4 to 5 minutes on each side. If you like, you can omit the spice rub and simply salt the chicken before grilling.

Mix:

1½ teaspoons fennel seeds
1½ teaspoons ground coriander
¾ teaspoon dry mustard
¾ teaspoon salt
¼ teaspoon ground cinnamon
¼ teaspoon ground red pepper

Rinse and pat dry, then rub the spice mixture all over:

4 bone-in chicken breast halves (with skin)

Heat 55 to 65 charcoal briquettes until covered with white ash. Spread the coals over one side of the grill to make a medium-hot fire. Replace the grill rack and cover the grill until the rack is hot, about 5 minutes. Place the chicken skin side down over the coals, cover the grill, and cook until the skin is crisp and golden brown, 8 to 10 minutes. Move the chicken to the opposite side of the grill and turn skin side up. Cover the grill and cook until the meat is opaque throughout, 10 to 15 minutes more. Meanwhile, mix in a small bowl:

¼ cup olive oil
¼ cup minced fresh cilantro or parsley or 1 tablespoon minced fresh thyme or oregano
3 tablespoons strained fresh lemon juice
1 small clove garlic, minced
¼ teaspoon salt

Remove the chicken to a serving platter, spoon the lemon-garlic oil over the pieces, and serve.

Grilled Chicken Dijon

4 servings

Mustard fanciers will argue the merits of a poupon *Dijon type in favor of sharp English, fiery Jamaican, or Chinese mustards, or vice versa. For this dish, however, those fanciers in the Dijon camp hold sway. Here, assertive but certainly not overstated Dijon mustard is balanced by olive oil, lemon, and garlic. These ingredients add interest, and the olive oil serves as a lubricant, protecting the mustard from burning on the grill. Let most of the marinade drain away from the chicken parts before grilling them.*

Rinse and pat dry:

3½ to 4½ pounds chicken parts

Mix in a large bowl:

⅓ cup olive oil
⅓ cup strained fresh lemon juice
3 tablespoons Dijon mustard
2 to 3 cloves garlic, minced
¾ teaspoon salt
½ teaspoon ground black pepper

Add the chicken pieces to the marinade and turn to coat well. Cover and refrigerate for 2 to 24 hours. Heat 55 to 65 charcoal briquettes until covered with white ash. Spread the coals over one side of the grill to make a medium-hot fire. Replace the grill rack and cover the grill until the rack is hot, about 5 minutes. Place the chicken parts skin side down directly over the coals and cook, moving the pieces around as needed to avoid charring, until the skin is crisp and golden, 8 to 10 minutes. Move the chicken opposite the coals and turn skin side up. Cover the grill and cook until the meat is opaque throughout, 10 to 15 minutes more.

Tandoori Chicken

4 servings

In Indian cooking, "tandoori" refers to cut-up chickens, meat kebabs, and flatbreads that are cooked in a tandoor, a fiercely hot, charcoal-fired vertical oven. Before cooking, chicken and meat are always marinated in an aromatic mixture of yogurt and spices. This marinade is tinted with a natural dye, which imparts to tandoori chicken (opposite) its characteristic orange-yellow color. An excellent tandoori-style chicken can be prepared in a covered grill using a very hot fire. To ensure that the outside does not char before the chicken cooks through, use the smallest chicken parts you can find or cut a 3½-pound chicken into parts yourself (see How to Cut Up a Chicken, 12). Two split rock Cornish hens also work well. In lieu of grilling, you can roast the chicken on a lightly oiled baking sheet in a 500°F oven for 25 to 30 minutes, but be prepared for a smoky kitchen.

Prepare:

Tandoori Marinade, 114

Remove the skin from:

3½ pounds chicken parts or 2 split rock Cornish hens

Add the chicken pieces to the marinade, turn to coat well, cover the bowl, and refrigerate for 4 to 6 hours. Prepare a hot charcoal fire. When the coals are covered with white ash, push them over to one side of the grill. Replace the grill rack and cover the grill until the rack is hot, about 5 minutes. Arrange the chicken parts bone side down on the hot rack over the coals, cover the grill, and cook for 15 minutes. Turn the chicken and place it opposite the coals, replace the grill cover, and cook until the juices run clear when the meat is pricked with a fork, 10 to 15 minutes more.

HABANERO

Reputed to be the hottest of all chilies, these lantern-shaped peppers pack tremendous fruity and floral flavors and aromas, along with an incredible punch. Usually found in markets colored green, yellow-orange, or bright orange, habaneros are sometimes mislabeled as the equally hot but less floral Scotch bonnet. Used extensively in the Yucatán, they measure about 1½ inches long and 1½ inches wide at the stem end.

Grill-Smoked Jamaican Jerk Chicken

6 to 8 servings

Chicken can be cooked in the unique Jamaican style known as "jerk." The cornerstone of all jerk dishes is a vinegary, intensely hot paste of dried herbs and habanero peppers, which are some five times hotter than jalapeños. If you cannot find these peppers, a habanero-based hot sauce makes a good substitute. You can cook the chicken immediately or marinate it, covered and refrigerated, for up to 12 hours.

Puree in a food processor or blender:

⅓ cup fresh lime juice

10 fresh habanero or Scotch bonnet peppers or ¼ cup habanero-based hot sauce

2 tablespoons white vinegar

2 tablespoons fresh orange juice

3 scallions, coarsely chopped

2 tablespoons dried basil

2 tablespoons dried thyme

2 tablespoons yellow mustard seeds or 1 tablespoon dry mustard

2 teaspoons ground allspice

1 teaspoon ground cloves

1 teaspoon salt

1 teaspoon ground black pepper

The mixture should have the consistency of thick tomato sauce. If needed, thin with additional:

Lime juice, vinegar, or orange juice

Rinse and pat dry, then brush this mixture over:

8 whole chicken legs, or 8 bone-in chicken breast halves (with skin)

Prepare a medium-hot charcoal fire. When the coals are covered with white ash, push them over to one side of the grill. Replace the grill rack. Arrange the chicken pieces skin side down opposite the coals. Cover the grill and cook for 20 minutes. Turn the chicken and cook until the meat is opaque throughout and pulls away from the bone, 30 to 60 minutes more, depending on the size of the chicken parts and the temperature of the fire.

ABOUT
FLAVOR
ENHANCERS

*A*n easy way to enhance the flavor of chicken is to season it with a savory mixture in the form of a dry rub, paste, or marinade before cooking. The chicken absorbs the essential oils from the herbs and spices, and when citrus juice, wine, or vinegar is used, the flesh of the bird becomes more tender. Fruity oils, sweetening sugar, and aromatic vegetables also contribute to a more vibrant, more intense taste.

Stock enhances flavor subtly. It is a vital ingredient in cooking, and no store-bought variety can compare with a well-tended homemade version. Stock is usually meant to be comparatively unassertive in flavor, so that it can be used for a number of purposes. The stock recipes featured here are used throughout the recipes in this book.

Clockwise from top: *Vinegar Marinade, 113; Beer Marinade, 113; White Wine Marinade, 113; Soy and Sherry Marinade, 114; Citrus Herb Marinade, 112*

Using Marinades

Marinades usually contain vinegar, lemon juice, or other acidic ingredient to tenderize the food as it soaks and to impart flavor. Marinades, especially those used on poultry, often include some olive oil, melted butter, or other fat in order to baste the food as it cooks.

To avoid making more marinade than you actually need, use a container just large enough to hold the food.

Tender foods like chicken can be marinated with delicious results, but avoid marinating it too long, or it will turn stringy, even mushy.

Refrigerate chicken while it marinates. Cubed pieces of poultry marinate for just 1 to 2 hours; bigger pieces proportionally longer.

Use a stainless-steel or wooden spoon to turn the chicken and to stir the marinade from time to time. A general rule is to allow 6 to 8 tablespoons of marinade for every 1 pound of chicken. Sometimes marinades are cooked first. Chill these before adding to the chicken, so they will not raise its temperature. Some marinades are also suitable as a finishing sauce. Marinades are usually best when prepared fresh. Vinaigrettes also make flavorful marinades.

Finally, sprinkling salt over the chicken before placing it in the marinade ensures that it is seasoned evenly. Chicken to be browned needs to be drained and patted dry after marinating; wet chicken will not brown properly. To intensify the full flavors of the marinade in the finished dish, use it as a braising liquid or to baste the food as it cooks. Just be sure to cook the marinade thoroughly by boiling first.

Citrus Herb Marinade

About ½ cup

This is among the simplest and most satisfying ways to give poultry lively flavor before applying heat.

Combine in a dish and blend with a fork:

¼ cup mild-tasting olive or nut oil
2½ tablespoons fresh lemon juice
1½ tablespoons fresh orange juice or dry red wine
⅓ cup chopped fresh parsley, preferably flat-leaf
1½ teaspoons dried thyme leaves or other appropriate herb
½ bay leaf, very finely crumbled
1 clove garlic, minced (optional)
1 teaspoon salt
¼ teaspoon ground black or white pepper, or to taste

Use immediately, or cover and refrigerate for up to 1 week.

MARINATING PRECAUTIONS

On a cautionary note, never use the marinade in which raw poultry has steeped for basting cooked food or as a sauce without first bringing it to a boil to kill any harmful bacteria from the raw food. It's important to remember to marinate only in glass, stainless steel, or food-grade plastic, so the container will not react with the acid.

QUICK CITRUS MARINADE

Prepare *Citrus Herb Marinade, above,* omitting the herbs and optional garlic, blending the oil, lemon juice, and orange juice or wine, then seasoning with salt and ground black or white pepper to taste. Use immediately. Marinate for 2 to 3 hours, turning the pieces often.

White Wine Marinade

About ¾ cup

Especially good with grilled or broiled poultry.

Whisk together thoroughly:

¼ cup white wine (it can be dry
   or fruity)
¼ cup vegetable oil
¼ cup minced shallots or onions
¾ teaspoon minced fresh tarragon,
   chervil, or thyme, or
   ¼ teaspoon dried
½ teaspoon ground white pepper
¼ teaspoon salt, or to taste

Let stand at room temperature for
1 hour to allow the flavor to
develop. Whisk to blend and use
immediately, or cover and refrigerate
for up to 1 week.

Vinegar Marinade

About 2¼ cups

A cooked marinade, traditionally used with game birds.

Combine in a medium saucepan
over low heat and simmer for
2 minutes:

2 cups water
¼ cup red wine vinegar
1 small onion (preferably red),
   thinly sliced
3 sprigs fresh parsley
2 sprigs fresh thyme
6 black peppercorns, cracked
6 whole allspice or juniper berries
2½ small bay leaves

Remove from the heat and season
with:

Salt to taste

Chill to use as a marinade. This
marinade will keep, covered and
refrigerated, for up to 1 week.

Beer Marinade

About 2 cups

A pungent mixture for broiling, grilling, and roasting.

Whisk together thoroughly:

1½ cups beer
¼ cup any citrus or ginger
   marmalade
1 tablespoon dry mustard
1 tablespoon minced peeled fresh
   ginger, or 1 teaspoon ground
2 cloves garlic, minced
¼ teaspoon salt
1 teaspoon sugar or honey

Use immediately, or cover and
refrigerate for up to 1 week.

Teriyaki Marinade

About 1 cup

Combine in a small saucepan over
medium heat and cook, stirring,
until the sugar is dissolved:

⅓ cup sake
⅓ cup mirin (sweet rice wine)
⅓ cup soy sauce, preferably
   low-sodium
2¼ teaspoons sugar

You can use the hot mixture immediately as a sauce, or chill it for a
marinade. The teriyaki will keep,
covered and refrigerated, for up to
1 month.

Soy and Sherry Marinade

About 1¼ cups

The combination of soy sauce and dry sherry produces an aromatic and delicious flavor in broiled or grilled chicken and game hens when marinated for only 2 to 3 hours.

Whisk together thoroughly:

½ cup soy sauce
½ cup dry sherry
2 tablespoons Dijon mustard
1 tablespoon hot red pepper sauce
¼ cup vegetable oil

Use immediately, or cover and refrigerate for up to 1 month.

Tandoori Marinade

About 1⅓ cups

In Indian cooking, chicken and other meats are always marinated in an aromatic mixture of yogurt and spices before they are cooked in a tandoor, a fiercely hot, charcoal-fire vertical oven. The acidity in the yogurt tenderizes the exterior of the meat and can actually overtenderize if left for more than 4 hours. This marinade is traditionally tinted with a natural dye, which imparts to tandoori chicken its characteristic orange-yellow color.

Whisk together thoroughly:

1 cup yogurt
2 to 3 tablespoons vegetable oil
2 teaspoons finely minced garlic
2 teaspoons finely minced peeled fresh ginger
1 teaspoon ground coriander
1 teaspoon ground cumin
1 teaspoon ground red pepper
1 teaspoon *Garam Masala*, 79, or ¼ teaspoon ground cinnamon
½ teaspoon ground turmeric
½ teaspoon salt
1 tablespoon yellow food coloring (optional)
1½ teaspoons red food coloring (optional)

Use immediately.

Using Dry Rubs and Pastes

A dry rub is a compatible blend of dried herbs and spices that is rubbed on whole birds or poultry pieces before cooking. When a dry rub is moistened with oil or ground fresh ginger or garlic, it becomes a paste, which is even easier to use, because it clings nicely.

Ingredients for rubs are ideally ground by hand with a mortar and pestle—there is less risk of overprocessing, and the herbs and spices seem to be most completely expressed. You can use a sturdy bowl and a wooden spoon if it suits you. The next most efficient tools are a spice grinder or coffee grinder or a blender. Their bowls are better shaped for small batches than those of a food processor; however, a good mini food processor can work. Pastes are best ground in a blender or food processor.

To use a dry rub or paste, simply rub the mixture over the entire surface of the bird or poultry piece, using enough pressure to make sure that an even layer adheres. Naturally, a mild mixture can be applied more thickly than one that is spicy or hot. (Wash your hands well after rubbing, as some spices can irritate the skin.)

Although a rub or paste smeared on just before cooking still adds flavor, apply it up to 24 hours before cooking, so the flavor will be more than skin deep. Turn the poultry several times as it rests, and leave the seasoning in place for cooking. (Some seasonings produce a handsome dark-colored finish and some create a tasty crunchy crust, especially in grilling or sautéing.)

Keep any unused rubs and pastes refrigerated for up to a week in tightly covered small jars. Discard any that have come into contact with raw poultry.

Thai Green Curry Paste

About 1 cup

This fragrant and spicy paste is excellent on poultry or stirred into soups, rice, pasta, and other grain dishes. Galangal, lemon grass, and shrimp paste are available in Asian markets. Combine in a small dry skillet over medium heat and toast, shaking the pan often to prevent burning, 2 to 3 minutes:

2 teaspoons coriander seeds
1 teaspoon cumin seeds
1 teaspoon fennel seeds
1 teaspoon black peppercorns

Remove from the heat, let cool to room temperature, and grind to a fine powder in a spice grinder, coffee grinder, or blender or with a mortar and pestle. Transfer to a small bowl.

Combine in a blender or food processor and process until finely chopped, about 4 minutes:

⅓ cup tightly packed fresh cilantro leaves
Two ¼-inch slices galangal or fresh ginger, peeled
1 stalk lemon grass, bottom third only, chopped
12 serrano peppers or 6 fresh jalapeño peppers, seeded and chopped
2 large shallots, chopped
4 cloves garlic, chopped
Grated zest of 1 lime
1 teaspoon shrimp paste (optional)
1½ teaspoons salt
1 teaspoon freshly grated or ground nutmeg

Add the spices and, with the machine running, slowly pour in:

¼ cup peanut oil

Cover and refrigerate until ready to use. This paste will keep, covered and refrigerated, for up to 1 week.

CUMIN SEEDS, GALANGAL, AND LEMON GRASS

From a plant native to the Nile Valley, cumin seeds are strong, hot, faintly bitter, with a touch of caraway. They should be roasted in a dry skillet before using whole or grinding into a powder.

Related to ginger, galangals come in two forms. Greater galangal's large rhizomes look like pale yellow ginger etched with thin crosswise stripes. In Thailand, their hot, ginger-pepper, sour flavor is preferred to ginger's. The texture is woody; pieces are thinly sliced (to be left, uneaten, on the plate) or finely pounded or grated. Select and store as for fresh ginger. Lesser galangal has a smaller rhizome with orange-red flesh and a stronger flavor. It is an ingredient in some bitters, liqueurs, and beers; in China, lesser galangal infusions are used medicinally. It is rarely available fresh. For an alternative use half ginger and half black pepper, in small amounts.

Lemon grass is an herb. Fresh lemon grass is sold by the stalk, which is gray-green, is 2 feet in length, and looks something like a scallion, though it is fibrous to the point of being woody. For this reason, unlike seasonings such as garlic and ginger, it is valued for the flavor it imparts rather than the substance it adds. Only the bulblike 6- to 8-inch base is used, after the top is trimmed and a layer of tough outer leaves is peeled off.

Cajun Dry Rub

About ¼ cup

This spice mix, best known as "black-ening spice," can be rubbed generously on chicken before pan broiling, grilling, or sautéing. It will transform into a tangy, deeply caramelized crust as the meat cooks. Expect the spices to smoke some during cooking. This mixture is much better than store bought.

Stir together well in a small bowl:

1 tablespoon cracked black peppercorns
1 tablespoon salt
2 teaspoons crushed fennel seeds
1 teaspoon dried thyme
1 teaspoon sweet or hot paprika
1 teaspoon dry mustard
1 teaspoon garlic powder
½ teaspoon ground red pepper
1 teaspoon ground sage

This rub will stay potent, covered and kept in a cool, dark, dry place, for up to 6 weeks.

Toasted Whole Spice Dry Rub

About 2 cups

This rub is delicious with rock Cornish hens.

Combine in a large dry skillet over medium heat and toast, shaking the pan often to prevent burning, until fragrant, 2 to 3 minutes:

Two 3-inch cinnamon sticks
8 cardamom pods
¼ cup white peppercorns
½ cup coriander seeds
¼ cup cumin seeds
1 tablespoon whole cloves
1 tablespoon whole allspice
2 small dried red chili peppers of your choice
4 whole star anise

Remove from the heat, let cool to room temperature, and grind to a fine powder in a spice grinder, coffee grinder, blender, or with a mortar and pestle. This rub will stay potent, covered and kept in a cool, dark, dry place, for up to 6 weeks.

West Indies Dry Rub

About 1 ¾ cups

This rub goes well on all kinds of poultry.

Combine in a small dry skillet over medium heat and toast, shaking the pan often to prevent burning, until fragrant, 2 to 3 minutes:

¼ cup cumin seeds
¼ cup coriander seeds

Remove from the heat. Let cool to room temperature, and grind to a fine powder in a spice grinder, coffee grinder, blender, or with a mortar and pestle. Transfer to a small bowl and add:

¼ cup curry powder
¼ cup ground white pepper
¼ cup ground ginger
¼ cup salt
2 tablespoons ground allspice
2 tablespoons ground red pepper

Stir together well. This rub will stay potent, covered and kept in a cool, dark, dry place, for up to 6 weeks.

Mediterranean Garlic Herb Paste

About 1 ½ cups

This paste is wonderful on grilled and roasted poultry. The garlic and red pepper flakes add a good deal of heat. Combine in a blender or food processor and coarsely puree, leaving the mixture a little chunky:

2 cups mixed fresh herbs (parsley, sage, rosemary, thyme, basil, and/or oregano)
10 cloves garlic
1 tablespoon red pepper flakes
½ cup olive oil
2 tablespoons salt
¼ cup cracked black peppercorns

Cover and refrigerate until ready to use. This paste will keep, covered and refrigerated, for up to 1 week.

Chili-Garlic Spice Paste

About 2 cups

This paste is good with poultry and vegetables. Use as little or as much jalapeño as you like. Combine in a blender or food processor until smooth:

¾ cup minced fresh jalapeño peppers
½ cup cloves garlic, peeled
½ cup olive oil
2 tablespoons grated lemon or lime zest
2 tablespoons cracked black peppercorns
1 tablespoon salt
2 teaspoons chili powder

Use immediately, or cover and refrigerate for up to 1 week.

Asian Ginger Spice Paste

About 2⅓ cups

This fragrant herb paste suits chicken, game birds, and roasted vegetables. Combine in a blender or food processor and coarsely puree, leaving the mixture a little chunky:

½ cup minced peeled fresh ginger
⅓ cup sesame oil
1 tablespoon red pepper flakes
¼ cup chopped fresh cilantro
¼ cup chopped fresh mint
¼ cup chopped fresh basil
2 tablespoons salt
2 tablespoons cracked white peppercorns

Cover and refrigerate until ready to use. This paste will keep, covered and refrigerated, for up to 1 week.

Mustard Paste

About ⅔ cup

This paste is delicious on chicken and gives a gilded finish. Using good-quality mustard is a must. We suggest using tarragon here, but fennel leaves are also a possibility. Brush the paste on sparingly to avoid burning during cooking. Stir together well in a small bowl:

½ cup Dijon or brown mustard, whole-grain or smooth
2 tablespoons dry white wine
1 clove garlic, minced (optional)
1 tablespoon minced fresh tarragon, or 1 teaspoon dried
1 teaspoon minced peeled fresh ginger, or ¼ teaspoon ground

Use immediately.

Using Bastes, Glazes, and Barbecue Sauces

A baste is a liquid that is brushed onto chicken during cooking. It is especially useful when the meat is exposed to high temperatures, as in roasting, grilling, and broiling. The simplest bastes to brush on are pan drippings, but anything that moistens can be used. Bastes should contain a good proportion of fat. Oil, butter, and drippings keep surfaces from drying out while contributing to a handsome, browned finish.

Seasonings add interest to a baste but are not necessary if surfaces have been seasoned before cooking. Avoid adding sweet ingredients (honey, sugar, fruit juice), since sugars scorch easily and may burn before the food is cooked.

Sweet ingredients do, however, belong in a glaze. A glaze is a liquid that adds luster and gloss to foods while cooking. The sheen comes from some form of melted sugar. Depending on the heat of the oven, the sweetness of the sauce, and the size of the piece of meat, apply a glaze during the last 15 to 45 minutes of cooking.

Glazes should be thick enough to paint on a surface without dripping. A quick final coating of glaze is often brushed on just before the food is served, and glazes can be passed as dipping sauces at the table. In addition to being sweet, glazes are typically fruity and/or spicy.

Barbecue sauces can be tomato-based or made with a variety of other ingredients. Although purists maintain that the only true barbecue is made with a dry spice rub, many prefer to add deep spicy flavor with a sauce. A form of glaze, barbecue sauce should be applied when you would a glaze—judging by the oven temperature, the sweetness of the sauce, and the size of the food. A nonsweet sauce can be brushed on from start to finish. Serve extra barbecue sauce—not used to baste during cooking—at the table.

Orange-Pineapple-Chipotle Baste

About 3 cups

This lively baste also makes a tasty marinade or dipping sauce for grilled poultry.

Combine in a medium saucepan over medium-high heat:

4 cups pineapple juice
2 cups orange juice
2 cups white vinegar
3 tablespoons pureed canned chipotle peppers, or to taste
2 tablespoons ground cumin

Bring to a boil, reduce the heat to medium, and simmer, uncovered, until reduced by about two-thirds, 45 to 60 minutes. Remove from the heat and stir in:

¼ cup fresh lime juice
½ cup chopped fresh cilantro
Salt and cracked black peppercorns to taste

Use hot or at room temperature. This baste will keep, covered and refrigerated, for about 1 month.

CHIPOTLE PEPPERS

Chipotle peppers (dried smoked jalapeños) have made great gains in popularity in this country for their intense, rich, smoky flavor. They show up everywhere, from canned tomato sauce (adobo) to salsas, sauces, pickles, stews, soups, and more. There are two types of chipotles, both made from different cultivars of the jalapeño. The first is the black-red chili chipotle (also know as the chipotle colorado, mora, or morita); this small chipotle (1 to 1½ inches long and ½ inch wide) is prized for its sweet, smoked flavor and its dark, rosewood red color. The second type, usually called chipotle meco, is larger (3 to 4 inches long by 1 inch wide) and pale brown in color, with a more tobacco-like taste and usually less heat.

To rehydrate dried chilies, cover the chilies with hot (not boiling) water, submerging the pieces in the bowl with a saucer, and letting them soak until pliant, 15 to 20 minutes.

Barbecue Sauce

About 2 cups

When cooking at high temperatures, apply this sauce during the last 15 minutes of cooking. This sauce works very well on chicken.

Combine in a medium saucepan over medium heat and cook, stirring often, until the sauce comes to a simmer:

1½ cups ketchup
1 cup cider vinegar or red wine vinegar
¼ cup Worcestershire sauce
¼ cup soy sauce
1 cup packed light or dark brown sugar

2 tablespoons dry mustard
4 tablespoons chili powder, or to taste
1 tablespoon grated, peeled fresh ginger, or 1 teaspoon ground
2 cloves garlic, minced
2 tablespoons vegetable oil
3 slices lemon

Simmer, stirring often, for 5 minutes. Remove the lemon slices if desired. This sauce will keep, covered and refrigerated, for up to 2 weeks.

Chipotle Pepper Barbecue Sauce

About 2 cups

This is a basic "all-purpose" sauce. We also use this as a basis for vinaigrettes, and to flavor mayonnaise. Try it on a grill-roasted whole bird.

Heat in a large saucepan over medium-high heat:

1 tablespoon olive oil

Add and cook, stirring, until lightly colored:

1 cup chopped onion
2 teaspoons minced garlic

Stir in, cover, and simmer until the chili peppers are very soft, about 30 minutes:

½ cup dried apricots, coarsely chopped
¾ cup dry white wine
¾ cup *Chicken Stock*, 124, or vegetable stock
½ cup fresh orange juice
2 large dried California or New Mexico (red Anaheim) peppers, seeded and torn into small pieces
1 or 2 dried or canned chipotle peppers, coarsely chopped

Let cool slightly and puree in a blender along with:

¼ cup pure maple syrup
2 tablespoons Dijon mustard

Strain through a fine-mesh sieve and season with:

Salt to taste

Depending on its use, if desired, thin with additional:

Stock or orange juice

Let cool to room temperature. This sauce will keep, covered and refrigerated, for up to 2 weeks.

Southwestern Apricot Glaze

About 1 cup

This sweet and spicy mixture works well on a wide variety of foods, but is particularly good brushed on chicken.

Combine in a small saucepan over medium heat:

1 cup apricot preserves
½ cup red wine vinegar
One 2-inch cinnamon stick, broken, or ¼ teaspoon ground cinnamon
2 tablespoons minced fresh chili peppers of your choice

Bring to a boil and cook until the mixture is slightly thickened, 5 to 7 minutes. Use hot or at room temperature. This glaze will keep, covered and refrigerated, for about 1 month.

Glazes for Roasted Poultry

Depending on size, wait until 15 to 30 minutes before the end of cooking to glaze poultry—the smaller the size, the shorter the time.

Brown Sugar: Mix ¾ cup packed light brown sugar and 2 teaspoons dry mustard. Slowly stir in fresh orange juice until of a spreading consistency.

Cranberry: Stir until blended and of a spreading consistency ¾ cup jellied cranberry sauce, ⅓ cup packed light brown sugar, and 1½ tablespoons fresh lemon juice, or to taste.

Mustard: Stir together ½ cup packed light brown sugar, ¼ cup yellow mustard, and 2 tablespoons honey or light molasses.

Clockwise from top: *Orange-Pineapple-Chipotle Baste, 119; Cajun Dry Rub, 117; Southwestern Apricot Glaze, above; Jamaican Jerk Paste (see Grill-Smoked Jamaican Jerk Chicken, 108); Chili-Garlic Spice Paste, 118*

Making Chicken Stock

Instead of calling for tender, young specimens, chicken stock is best made with the bones and meat of older birds, cooked slowly for a long time to extract every vestige of flavor. By definition, stock is made with more bones than meat. Broth, on the other hand, is made from more meat than bones.

The characteristics of any good stock are flavor, body, and clarity. Of the three, flavor is paramount, and the way to get it is by using a high proportion of ingredients to water. The most flavorful stocks are made with only enough water to cover the ingredients. Additional water is needed only when it evaporates below the level of the ingredients before the stock is fully cooked. Follow the recipe for ideal ratios of liquid to solids, but the principle is simple: Keep the solids covered with water while cooking.

Cooking times for stocks depend on how long it takes to extract all the flavor from the ingredients. It will take at least 4 hours for raw chicken bones to give up all their richness.

When preparing ingredients for stock making, it is important to chop bones and vegetables to size according to their cooking times—large for long cooking and small for quick cooking—to allow their flavors to be fully extracted.

Simmering the stock past the recommended cooking time can produce an unpleasant bitter taste. A stock should be strained when all the flavors and goodness have been fully extracted from the bones, meat, and vegetables. If in doubt, retrieve a bone with some meat attached from the simmering stock. If the meat still has some flavor, allow the stock to simmer for longer. If the meat is entirely tasteless and the bone joints are falling apart, it is time to strain the stock.

If a stock tastes weak after straining, remove and discard the fat, then simmer the stock briskly to reduce the water content and concentrate the flavor. This technique, known as reduction and used extensively in sauce making, does produce a more deeply flavored stock, but in the process much of the aromatic, fresh taste of the vegetables is lost. Bear in mind that a light stock is sometimes more appropriate for its subtlety. In instances when you want a hearty stock, roast the bones and vegetables before adding them to the stock pot.

Bones add body to a stock, while meat adds flavor. Bones contain gelatin, which gives stock body and a rich, smooth texture. Always use a combination of bones and meat. Raw ingredients produce the best stock, but in a pinch, leftover meat and vegetables will do. Leftover carcasses, broken up and pushed under the water, make a fine stock.

The clarity of a stock is more than an aesthetic concern. A clear stock tastes clean and fresh, while a cloudy stock will often seem greasy and muddled. The secret to a clear stock is to start with cold water, allow it to come slowly to a boil, then immediately lower the temperature to the slightest simmer while you carefully skim any impurities, froth, or fat that rises to the surface. If stock is permitted to boil, these impurities will be incorporated into the liquid instead of the foam.

THE STOCKPOT

The most important tool for making stock is the most obvious—a stockpot. The best type of stockpot is narrow, tall, and heavy-bottomed, to allow the stock to simmer gently without too much evaporation and to facilitate skimming. An 8- to 10-quart stockpot is ideal for making 2- to 4-quart batches of stock. Be sure the pot is large enough to accommodate all of the solids (bones or whole carcasses and vegetables) with room to cover them with 2 inches of water. Remember to avoid aluminum pots, which may react with the ingredients and affect the flavor. A second large pot is handy for cooling strained stock; plastic containers will also work, but they insulate, and so the stock will not cool as quickly.

RULES FOR MAKING STOCK

● The higher the ratio of solids to water, the more flavorful the stock. The water should just barely cover the ingredients. Too much water will make a watery stock. Add water during cooking if necessary.

● Cut the ingredients into small pieces for quick-cooking stocks and larger pieces for long-cooking stocks. Ingredients for poultry stocks should be cut into medium pieces.

● Start with cold water and bring it slowly to a simmer. Never rush a stock. Simmer gently so bubbles just barely break on the surface. Never allow a stock to boil.

● Skim the impurities that rise to the surface as the stock simmers—often during the first 30 minutes, and then once an hour or so. Have two bowls nearby, one filled with water to set the skimmer in so that it does not get covered with congealed fat and impurities, and a second bowl to collect what you skim off.

● Stop cooking the stock when there is no flavor left in the ingredients.

● Adjust the flavor. If the stock tastes too thin, simmer it until it is flavorful. As the water evaporates, the stock reduces in volume and its flavor concentrates. Vegetable stock becomes bitter when overreduced.

● A well-made stock contains very little fat. Begin by trimming all meat and bones of visible fat, and finish by either skimming the stock carefully while still warm or chilling the stock so the fat forms a solid layer and is easily removed. Alternatively, and easiest yet, use an inexpensive gravy separator.

● Many variables affect the yield of a stock recipe, such as the size of the pot and the kind of meat or bones used. Ultimately, a good flavor is more important than achieving the exact yield.

Chicken Stock

About 8 cups

Stock is an important part of cooking. No store-bought variety can compare with a well-tended homemade stock. Using the lesser amount of chicken suggested here will result in a lighter stock, which will reinforce the flavor in many dishes without adding a pronounced chicken taste; the greater amount will yield a richer one, to give backbone to soups and sauces.

Combine in a stockpot over medium heat:

4 to 5½ pounds chicken parts (backs, necks, wings, legs, or thighs), or 1 whole 4- to 5½-pound roasting chicken, well rinsed

16 cups cold water (or just enough to cover)

Bring to a boil, reduce the heat, and simmer gently. Skim often until impurities no longer appear, about 30 minutes. Add:

1 onion, coarsely chopped

1 carrot, peeled and coarsely chopped

1 celery stalk, coarsely chopped

1 *Bouquet Garni*, opposite

Simmer, uncovered, for 3 hours, adding water as needed to cover. Strain into a clean pot or heatproof plastic container. Let cool, uncovered, then refrigerate. Remove the fat when ready to use.

STRAINING AND STORING STOCK

When stock has finished cooking, strain it through a fine-mesh sieve (or a colander lined with a double layer of cheesecloth) into another pot or a large heatproof container and discard the solids. Do not let the stock sit out at room temperature for long as it is a good breeding ground for bacteria. Speed up the cooling process by placing the hot pot, uncovered, in a sink of ice water and stirring it. Once the stock cools enough so that it will not raise the temperature of your refrigerator, cover it tightly and chill it. When the stock is chilled, fat will rise in a solid mass that must be removed before reheating. While cold, this fat layer actually protects the stock. Stock will keep for 3 to 5 days in the refrigerator. If refrigerated for longer, after 3 days skim the solidified fat from the surface and boil the stock for 10 minutes, then refrigerate it for another 3 to 5 days. For prolonged storage, transfer stock to plastic containers or plastic freezer bags and freeze it. Small amounts of stock can also be frozen in ice cube trays.

Bouquet Garni

Since herbs tend to float and get in the way as you skim the surface of a stock, we recommend tying them together in a little packet, known as a bouquet garni. Vary the contents to suit your dish, with additions such as whole cloves, dill, lemon zest, or garlic. For express broth or quick-cooking stocks, there is no need to tie the seasonings in a bundle— they may simply be tossed in with the vegetables.

Wrap in a 4 × 4-inch piece of cheesecloth:

Small bunch of parsley or parsley stems
8 sprigs fresh thyme, or 1 teaspoon dried
1 bay leaf
2 or 3 celery leaves (optional)

Tie the cheesecloth securely with a piece of kitchen string or omit the cheesecloth and simply tie the herbs together at their stems.

Refrigerate in a tightly covered container until ready to use.

BROWN (OR ROASTED) CHICKEN STOCK

This chicken stock variation has a richer flavor than "white" chicken stock.

Preheat the oven to 425°F. Prepare *Chicken Stock, opposite,* by combining all ingredients except the water and bouquet garni, in a heavy roasting pan and roasting, stirring occasionally, until well browned, about 1 hour. Remove the chicken and vegetables to a stockpot and deglaze the hot roasting pan by adding 1 cup water and scraping up any browned bits. Add the liquid to the pot along with water to cover, about 16 cups, and the bouquet garni. Continue as directed.

SEASONING STOCK

Stocks are usually meant to be comparatively unassertive in flavor, so that they can be used for a number of purposes. Onions, carrots, and celery, the traditional mixture of aromatic vegetables for stock, known as a *mirepoix* in French, should be added sparingly about 30 minutes after the stock has begun to simmer and the impurities have been removed. Different styles of cooking alter this classic mixture. Mushrooms and leeks are also common. The discreet use of either fresh or dried seasonings, including parsley, thyme, bay leaves, and peppercorns, in the form of a bouquet garni, left, is equally important. Salt is almost never added to stock. The reduction process, during both the original simmering and any subsequent cooking, would concentrate the salt and ruin the results.

Index

ACKNOWLEDGMENTS

Special thanks to my wife and editor in residence, Susan; our indispensable assistant and comrade, Mary Gilbert; and our friends and agents, Gene Winick and Sam Pinkus. Much appreciation also goes to Simon & Schuster, Scribner, and Weldon Owen for their devotion to this project. Thank you Carolyn, Susan, Bill, Marah, John, Terry, Roger, Gaye, Val, Norman, and all the other capable and talented folks who gave a part of themselves to the Joy of Cooking All About series.

My eternal appreciation goes to the food experts, writers, and editors whose contributions and collaborations are at the heart of Joy—especially Stephen Schmidt. He was to the 1997 edition what Chef Pierre Adrian was to Mom's final editions of Joy. Thank you one and all.

Ethan Becker

FOOD EXPERTS, WRITERS, AND EDITORS

Selma Abrams, Jody Adams, Samia Ahad, Bruce Aidells, Katherine Alford, Deirdre Allen, Pam Anderson, Elizabeth Andoh, Phillip Andres, Alice Arndt, John Ash, Nancy Baggett, Rick and Deann Bayless, Lee E. Benning, Rose Levy Beranbaum, Brigit Legere Binns, Jack Bishop, Carole Bloom, Arthur Boehm, Ed Brown, JeanMarie Brownson, Larry Catanzaro, Val Cipollone, Polly Clingerman, Elaine Corn, Bruce Cost, Amy Cotler, Brian Crawley, Gail Damerow, Linda Dann, Deirdre Davis, Jane Spencer Davis, Erica De Mane, Susan Derecskey, Abigail Johnson Dodge, Jim Dodge, Aurora Esther, Michele Fagerroos, Eva Forson, Margaret Fox, Betty Fussell, Mary Gilbert, Darra Goldstein, Elaine Gonzalez, Dorie Greenspan, Maria Guarnaschelli, Helen Gustafson, Pat Haley, Gordon Hamersley, Melissa Hamilton, Jessica Harris, Hallie Harron, Nao Hauser, William Hay, Larry Hayden, Kate Hays, Marcella Hazan, Tim Healea, Janie Hibler, Lee Hofstetter, Paula Hogan, Rosemary Howe, Mike Hughes, Jennifer Humphries, Dana Jacobi, Stephen Johnson, Lynne Rossetto Kasper, Denis Kelly, Fran Kennedy, Johanne Killeen and George Germon, Shirley King, Maya Klein, Diane M. Kochilas, Phyllis Kohn, Aglaia Kremezi, Mildred Kroll, Loni Kuhn, Corby Kummer, Virginia Lawrence, Jill Leigh, Karen Levin, Lori Longbotham, Susan Hermann Loomis, Emily Luchetti, Stephanie Lyness, Karen MacNeil, Deborah Madison, Linda Marino, Kathleen McAndrews, Alice Medrich, Anne Mendelson, Lisa Montenegro, Cindy Mushet, Marion Nestle, Toby Oksman, Joyce O'Neill, Suzen O'Rourke, Russ Parsons, Holly Pearson, James Peterson, Marina Petrakos, Mary Placek, Maricel Presilla, Marion K. Pruitt, Adam Rapoport, Mardee Haidin Regan, Peter Reinhart, Sarah Anne Reynolds, Madge Rosenberg, Nicole Routhier, Jon Rowley, Nancy Ross Ryan, Chris Schlesinger, Stephen Schmidt, Lisa Schumacher, Marie Simmons, Nina Simonds, A. Cort Sinnes, Sue Spitler, Marah Stets, Molly Stevens, Christopher Stoye, Susan Stuck, Sylvia Thompson, Jean and Pierre Troisgros, Jill Van Cleave, Patricia Wells, Laurie Wenk, Caroline Wheaton, Jasper White, Jonathan White, Marilyn Wilkenson, Carla Williams, Virginia Willis, John Willoughby, Deborah Winson, Lisa Yockelson.

Weldon Owen wishes to thank the following people for their generous assistance and support in producing this book: Desne Border, Ken DellaPenta, and Joan Olson.